THE SPIRITUAL EXERCISES

How They Helped Me Discover Myself and God Over 40 Years

REV. TOM DONOHUE

◆ FriesenPress

One Printers Way
Altona, MB R0G 0B0
Canada

www.friesenpress.com

Copyright © 2024 by Rev. Tom Donohue
First Edition — 2024

All rights reserved.

No part of this publication may be reproduced in any form, or by any means, electronic or mechanical, including photocopying, recording, or any information browsing, storage, or retrieval system, without permission in writing from FriesenPress.

ISBN
978-1-03-917560-0 (Hardcover)
978-1-03-917559-4 (Paperback)
978-1-03-917561-7 (eBook)

1. RELIGION, CHRISTIAN RITUALS & PRACTICE, WORSHIP & LITURGY

Distributed to the trade by The Ingram Book Company

Endorsements

Tom Donohue's highly personal explication of the exercises of Saint Ignatius is rich with insight, wisdom, and analogies to help us deepen our spiritual journey. We come to appreciate the different ways to pray and experience our prayers in our heart, as God moves into us and we move into God.

— Gail D. Storey, author of *I Promise Not to Suffer: A Fool for Love Hikes the Pacific Crest Trail*

Toward the end of his reflections on the Spiritual Exercises, Fr. Tom expresses his greatest desire that what he has shared will help the reader see God acting in their life and become more conscious of the divine presence. I would submit that Fr. Tom facilitates this reaching "up" to God by getting down to earth, especially by sharing his own experiences in a highly relatable way. I'm certain that, like me, many readers will find that Fr. Tom's personal approach helps them to connect more personally to God.

— Br. Peter Poel, O.F.M. Cap.

A reading of Father Tom's personal encounter with the Spiritual Exercises is inspiring. Most of all, he convincingly reveals how this four week journey, graced with faith, humility, and perseverance, gifts us with a close and loving relationship with Christ. His stories, experiences and rich examples of the spiritual life are a clear reminder that, like the Jesuits, we too can "find God in all things".

— Angela Townsend, MSW, RS
   Assistant Professor and Toldo Research Chair for the Advancement of Human Formation
   St. Peter's Seminary, London, ON

Fr. Thomas Donohue understands our shared human need to grow in the gifts of the first weeks of the Spiritual Exercises of St. Ignatius. Based on 40 years of personal reflection on the exercises, Fr. Donohue demonstrates a personal humility that reveals the wisdom of the Spiritual Exercises and therefore becomes an approachable personal guide for all the spiritual exercises. This book challenges us to return to the basic self-understanding and healing that the Spiritual Exercises offer.

— Fr. Peter Keller

Table of Contents

Introduction 1

The Exercises 13

The First Week 31

Second Week 53

Third Week 69

Fourth Week 81

Spiritual Exercising 89

Acknowledgements 101

Introduction

This little book is meant to share a few reflections I have found by trying to follow Jesus with the help of the Spiritual Exercises written by St. Ignatius of Loyola five hundred years ago. It is not a guide of how to do the Spiritual Exercises, but it might pique your curiosity enough to interest you into doing these exercises. There is a format of course, but one should embark on the journey with a competent guide. The exercises are not something one can do by oneself. There are too many possible options that will crop up on the journey. Frodo had many difficult passages in the *Lord of the Rings*, but without Gandalf intervening, Middle Earth might not have survived. And it is the same with these exercises. If you embark on them, you will spend many hours in silence, peering deeply into your heart searching for God, but it will be important to spend some time regularly with a Spiritual Director to avoid pitfalls. As we open to the Spirit of God, we need to watch for the spirit of the enemy of humanity as well. The exercises can help one learn to distinguish the two spirits from one another, but even today I sometimes miss the signs of the enemy Ignatius warns against, so I do not advise anyone going to search for God without a good Spiritual Director. I have directed people on parts of their journey toward God, but I would be a fool if I directed myself without a guide.

Now you may wonder who I am, and what started me on the journey to find Jesus. Church had been a big part of my life as a child, but leaving my small town and moving to Toronto had helped me become a lapsed Catholic. In my late twenties there was a young lady who I wanted to get to know better, and I found out that she attended a mass followed by a potluck supper weekly. I figured I should go there to get to know her better. I tried to arrive for the end of the mass but in time for supper. Around the third or fourth week, God had a surprise for me. The venue had changed, and the mass started very late. When I walked into the room, I had no inkling my life was about to change forever.

Now the church of my childhood had been very regimented, and I was surprised to find myself in the Oak Room at the Newman Centre with folks gathered around a small table that served as an altar. A priest sat there, praying in English, not Latin, facing the folks gathered around watching him attentively. I did not see any one person quietly mouthing the prayers of the Rosary while he celebrated. And at communion, there were no lines or rails, but a lay minister brought the Eucharist to us where we were. I was not sure if I should even accept it, as I was not sure it was Jesus, but something in me reached out, and as I received communion, I suddenly realized what it meant to be loved and accepted, and I knew I had received Jesus and that he loved me unconditionally. To

The Spiritual Exercises

tell you the truth, I do not remember anything else of that night. I had walked into the room not believing in the real presence and have not doubted it for a minute since.

A day or two later, I went to talk to Father John about how Jesus was really present in the Eucharist. He listened patiently for a while—he was a very holy, spiritual guy, I would discover—and then asked what I knew about Jesus. I had to admit my knowledge of Jesus was incomplete. He gave me an old RSV Bible and said, "Read about him." I took the Bible home, a little discouraged, not thinking that there would be this much work to meeting Jesus, but willing to give it a shot. When I got home, I remembered that Jesus was discussed in what we used to call the New Testament, and most of the Bible was Old Testament. Also, the Gospels, which told the story of Jesus, were just part of it. And I was even happier to see that the Gospel of Mark was the shortest Gospel, so I figured I would at least check it out.

The Gospel of Mark had me hooked. I was surprised at how much of it I knew from just going to mass as a child. I had never read the Bible, but I had heard the stories. Next up were Matthew and Luke. They had the story Mark told, but each had added details to flesh out their points. John had a way of telling the story differently. I, of course, at that time had no idea, but I had ended up reading the Gospels in the order that they were written. I also knew instinctively that they were all writing about someone who had entered deeply into their lives. Jesus had interacted with each differently, relating to them as individuals. I could not have articulated it clearly, but I began to see that Jesus, who had overwhelmed me with love at the mass, would reveal himself to me. And the Jesus I would meet would be the Jesus they had met, but as each of the four evangelists' hearts were touched by Jesus in a way that was unique to them, so my encounter would be unique as well. I remember a friend saying once that my siblings and I had different mothers. I thought she was a little crazy. Then she went on to do good impressions of how we all talked to our mother. She was right—this one lady had become the mother each of our relationships needed. In the same way, this one Jesus has been a billion different persons for his followers. When Paul speaks of being all things for all people, he was being a true follower of Jesus.

I continued reading the Bible. After the Christian Scriptures were finished, I went on to read the Jewish Scriptures as well. I did not understand much, and after forty years I still get insights from that book that had seemed so intimidating. I became what some people refer to as a revert. I attended mass, even played in the choir sometimes, got involved with Development and Peace, helped our church sponsor some of the Vietnamese boat people, and found my life changing in ways that I found positive. I thought I had found God, but Jesus had one other surprise up his sleeve.

It happened at a midnight mass on Christmas Eve. The mass on that day is special. I was not singing, just part of the congregation, and I was enjoying the celebration. There were four priests gathered around the altar at the Newman Centre that night, and suddenly I noticed Jesus was there with them. He looked directly at me, and as I looked back, I knew I was being told that the Eucharist was going to be our point of contact. We would be together for life, and God would share my life through this sacrament. I do not know how I knew

The Spiritual Exercises

any of that, but I do know that for over forty years, in many places in many countries on different continents, I have connected with God through the Eucharist. And I also know that accountant I was trying to be then had no idea where the gaze that night would lead.

Now before you get worried that this might turn into a book of visions and such, these two experiences that kickstarted my walk with Jesus were the only semi-mystical experiences I had. They were pure grace. I did not ask for them. They were what Ignatius describes as the best and easiest way God lets us know an answer, even if we do not know we had a question. Most decisions he talks about in the second week are more complex. But they did call for a response. In some ways, my falling in love with Jesus, who loved me first, was like my father and mother. He fell in love with her when he met her at a dance. It was not as quick for her. But he knew love was calling him into something new. He even wrote his sister to tell her he had met the girl he was going to marry. There is no evidence she wrote her brother to discuss her upcoming nuptials, but marry they did, and four children came from it, plus twelve grand- and great-grandchildren, most of whom he met. I had no idea where this love I had discovered would lead. But my father had pursued his love; I knew I had to follow mine as well. And God was about to begin to show how I would be able to follow that path.

Now I had to decide how to follow Jesus. Since the Eucharist seemed to be my point of contact, I thought maybe this was a call to the priesthood. I knew nothing about how to do that, but I did some research, contacted a few religious orders, and thought maybe the Jesuits would be the way to go. Do not ask me why that seemed to make sense. I knew Oblates, Basilians, and even some diocesan priests, and no Jesuits, but I did like Bernard Lonergan's writings and had been impressed by Karl Rahner's book on prayer. Whatever my reasoning, I started meeting with their vocation director, who set me up with a Spiritual Director for the first time in my life. Fr. Larry helped over the year to discern my vocation and used some of the discernment methods found in the Spiritual Exercises, and while I did not do the formal exercises at that time, I got my first taste of Ignatian Spirituality and liked it a lot. I also started going to mass before work and found out that was difficult in Toronto, as most masses were at 9:00 a.m., but I found one I could attend. My love of this way of praying really started that year.

After a little over a year, I applied, but the priests I met with thought I might be more interested in a L'Arche community. I might have been had I ever heard of them, so Fr. Bill A., the vocation director, sent me to visit Fr. Bill C., who had spent time in a community in France. After a nice visit drinking tea and swatting flies on the porch of the farm community where he lived, I was interested, so my next stop was Stratford. After a few visits, I decided I would move in. Marjorie, the director, thought I should try it for a month before deciding, and I said fine, but I was quitting my job as an accountant and getting rid of my apartment because I was sure at least that part of my life was over. I had done three shorter visits before taking this step. I would not be going back if things did not work out. I packed up my clothes, got rid of my furniture, and moved to Stratford for at least a month. Thus began my next phase of getting to know Jesus.

The Spiritual Exercises

My time in Stratford was a truly graced period in my life. The few years I had spent growing in my faith week by week at the Newman Centre in Toronto had slowly brought about changes in how I lived my life and had brought a new freedom to my soul. God was wise enough to know I needed to heal myself of various things before I could venture from being someone who enquired about Jesus and followed some of his teachings to finding out if I could become a disciple. Richard Rohr has said a way to find Jesus is to step out of your comfort zone and discover life and God at the fringes of society. Moving into a community where most had developmental delays fit the bill for me. Jean Vanier has said that the work of L'Arche was to change the world one heart at a time, and now was my heart's turn to change.

The time in Stratford was truly a time of change and growth for me. There were struggles, of course. After years of working for a large developer in Toronto, in Stratford I found myself in a different place, living at a different pace. But there was an intensity there. In my past life we worked to make the company a success, of course, but it was to bring us individual rewards. Now success was not measured in dollars but in growth in relationships. There was work, but the real work was seeing how each member, regardless of abilities, could find a meaningful place to make the whole thing work. I did a few things well. They even let me be the Executive Director for a bit, but the rewards came in other things.

One small example: I was walking down the street with John, a man about thirty years old, when he said with pride, "This is John Street, the same as my name." It was exciting to be with someone who was discovering that the work he had done to learn to read was suddenly helping him learn more about his world. He may never read the books I have read, but he had discovered one more way to navigate the world independently. In some way I have experienced this with Spiritual Exercises. Over the years, I found how to apply more and more of these exercises, and now find they help me see the road signs God gives me for living my life. John discovered he was on John Street. Often God has helped me discover where I am on my spiritual journey through working on what I have learned from these exercises.

It was while in Stratford that I negotiated one of the difficult transitions in my life. My father died. It was not an easy time, but there were moments of grace involved. It was the closest I had come to death. I had known other deaths, of course, but this death I saw up close and could catch glimpses of God moving closer to my father as he slowly moved toward God and a new life. I knew I needed to know more about this God who had lived this passage with our family. It was now time to decide if L'Arche was to be my life's work. It was time to do The Spiritual Exercises. For many practical reasons, I chose to do the exercises using Annotation 19, where you do the work for a little over an hour daily for around a year. It also involved weekly trips to Guelph to meet with Bill G. It was in that year my walk with Jesus reached a new level of intensity. At first, I thought I was being called to marriage, but that was not the call, and I decided that maybe besides knowing God I should focus a little on knowing about God. So, at the end of my term as director, I resigned and went to do a sabbatical at Regis College in Toronto.

The Spiritual Exercises

I had studied Business Computing Systems and Accounting and had participated in courses designed by the Thomas More Institute in Toronto, but this was the year that I thought about God in a more systematic way, even wrote essays and such. Oddly enough, it was the course I took on Hindu Christian Dialogue that got me the deepest into my Catholic faith. (I even did a sixty-page essay on that one.) You of course learn about the Spiritual Exercises by doing them, but at Regis I did a Spiritual Direction practicum and learned some of the techniques one can employ to help others searching for God, using some of the wisdom of the Spiritual Exercises where appropriate. These five-hundred-year-old exercises were becoming more central to me as I continued my walk with Jesus.

After Regis, I decided to return to L'Arche, this time to work with the community in Ottawa. Even though I had grown up in Quebec, my French was far from stellar, so a bilingual community presented some challenges, but again God had a gift for me there. When I was growing up in Quebec there was a myth that somehow there was a fundamental difference between the French and the English. In Ottawa I learnt that just as there was nothing separating people with developmental delays from others, identities like French, English, Irish, Dutch, African, you name it, all mean nothing for a follower of Christ. St. Paul had figured it out very early on (Galatians 3:28–29), but it took me walking with Jesus for almost ten years to finally understand—God's love is for all.

So although it had taken about ten years, God—who had started drawing me to him in the person of Jesus with a discussion about the book *Insight* (kind of ironic when I think about it)—had hit me over the head with overpowering love in the Eucharist, had called me back to Church, to Stratford, to Regis College, and Ottawa, and had finally healed my heart enough that maybe he could do something with me. After almost two years in Ottawa, I awoke in my room in the basement knowing it was time to look at the priesthood again. What followed were phone calls and meetings, which ended with me entering St. Peter's Seminary days after my fortieth birthday. Then on May 3, 1997, at forty-eight years old, I was ordained as a priest for the Diocese of London. I continued to practice Ignatian spirituality in the seminary and as a priest for twenty-five years with the help of Jesuits in Guelph and Pickering in Ontario and in Sedalia, Colorado. I did the exercises again, this time over a thirty-day retreat, and got more Spiritual Direction hints from a course run by Institute for Priestly Formation (not all Jesuit-run, but much helpful material).

I have gone on a bit about my journey to show first why I love these exercises so much, but also to show that the walk with God is often a meandering one, with twists and turns. The more you live the Spirituality, the more change will come. Ignatius never imagined he was designing a system of prayers that you did for thirty days and then went on with your life. As we look at them, I hope you will see they are a system that can be adapted for each person. Many do not realize that the twelve steps in Alcoholics Anonymous are a successful modern adaptation, but even they sometimes get adapted. I remember once chatting with a man who had been sober twelve years. I asked him if he had done the steps more

The Spiritual Exercises

than once, as many do. He said they were too complicated; he just used the slogans and the meetings. Hard to argue with him. He took what he needed from the fellowship and had gotten sober. So let us look at various aspects of these exercises. There might be one or two practices you might wish to incorporate into your prayer life. And who knows, some day you might seek out a guide to lead you through these exercises as you negotiate some parts of your life. Whatever you do with what you find here, I hope you follow Ignatius's advice and do it all for the greater glory of God.

The Exercises

Ignatius starts his Spiritual Exercises with a prayer that probably predates him, although it is often attributed to him. This prayer is a favourite prayer for many. In the traditional translations, the prayer is addressed to the Soul of Christ. This is the closest Ignatius comes to mentioning the Holy Spirit in his Spiritual Exercises. He discovered talking too much about the Holy Spirit landed him in prison from time to time in his days, which might be why the Holy Spirit is not named in the Spiritual Exercises. However, you will find the Spirit between the lines quite often. This prayer was a favourite of Ignatius and was no doubt one of his simplest exercises. David L. Fleming, SJ, along with John English, SJ, led a revival of Ignatian Spirituality after Vatican II, and his book *Draw Me into Your Friendship* includes a beautiful contemporary reading of this prayer:

Jesus ... Best Friend

Jesus … Best Friend
may your soul give life to me,
may your flesh be food for me,
may you warm my hardened heart.

Jesus … Best Friend
may your tears now wash me clean,
may your passion keep me strong,
may you listen to my plea.

Jesus … Best friend
may your wounds take in my hurts,
may your gaze be fixed on me,
may I not betray your love

Jesus … Best Friend
may you call me at death's door
may you hold me close to you,
may you place me with God's saints,
may I ever sing your praise. Amen. !

The Spiritual Exercises

Fleming's contemporary reading of the Anima Christi illustrates clearly how Ignatius saw that friendship with Jesus is our source, our nourishment, our healing, and how following our Good Shepherd will lead us to heaven. It is that vision of our Best Friend Jesus that might have inspired these words in Vatican II:

> We believe that the Eucharist is the "source and summit of the Christian life" in that the Eucharist is the culmination of God's saving actions in Jesus Christ and our worship and union with Him who leads us to the Father in the power of the Holy Spirit. [2]

Now Ignatius certainly saw the value of Christ's continued presence among us and nourishing us in the Eucharist (a Greek word meaning *thanksgiving*, which Catholics use to describe Communion), but I believe he, being involved in the Counter-Reformation, saw intuitively that the mass was our mission statement. Shortly after his death, the Tridentine Mass (the Latin Mass Catholics celebrated for five hundred years) was instituted with its beautiful stark ending: *Ite, Missa est*—Go, your Mission is or Go, the Mass is. The words were an inspiration to Avery Dulles. It is too bad that his suggestion to just leave them hanging in the air without any explanation was not taken. Often today you hear something like Go in peace, glorifying God with your life, which takes away the simple GO. He envisioned everyone leaving with these words in their heart, no songs or fanfare; we have received our friend Jesus, now we are now being sent to do his will. His exercises were suggestions of ways we could encounter God, be inspired, and do what Jesus desires us to do as he watches our life with his gaze fixed on us. Ignatius wanted the laity of his day to meet their friend Jesus, know their friend Jesus, receive his love and mercy, and allow their friend to guide them to their final destiny—eternity with God.

Ignatius then moves on to various annotations or notes for the exercises. The first note is quite simple. He says we need to remember that exercises are of various kinds. In physical exercises, we do different things. My exercise routine today at seventy-two is quite different from what it was at twenty. It is the same with Spiritual Exercises. There are different ways of praying, and there are different ways of experiencing our prayer. Ignatius says that during these exercises, we will encounter many ways to pray. He also points out in the second annotation that we must also know who the director is. The director offers suggestions, passages for us to pray with, but the director is not to offer interpretations. As we pray, we should remember that the interpretation must be ours. The director might suggest where to look for our encounter with God. The director's role is not to try and force certain thoughts or ideas into our heads from the passages but to give us passages where we might come to know and encounter God. In Catholicism, very few Gospel passages have been definitively defined. If you do not believe me, try watching five homilies from a broadcast television Sunday Mass, and see how the same three readings and one psalm have stirred each preacher in unique ways. The director is not there to teach you what he has learned but to hear from you the next day what you have learned.

The Spiritual Exercises

The third annotation is particularly important. Ignatius points out that sometimes when we pray, we are meditating and thinking deeply. That is a good thing. But at other times, the readings may appear as deep emotions, not well-formed thoughts. Feelings of being loved, feelings of sorrow, or feelings of joy—whatever the feelings we should experience it deeply. Sometimes the feeling is what God wants us to have, not the reason for it. Ignatius puts stock in following our emotions during these exercises. He reminds us that whether the readings we are contemplating and meditating on are inspiring thoughts or emotions, we should always be reverent because the thoughts or the emotions are gifts from God to us. God is moving us in ways we may not understand. One truth I have learned following this type of prayer is that I may never understand much about the God who created the universe, but I have learned how deeply I am loved by that God, and that God has guided my life for many years.

The fourth annotation is where Ignatius explains the basic structure of the exercises. He talks about the exercises being four weeks, but tells us to think of them more as four movements in the Spirit. The first week or segment of the exercises is where we marvel in the love that God has for us and grapple with the times that we have failed to respond lovingly to God. We learn that we sometimes need forgiveness for the things we have done in our own lives. The second week, or the second movement, moves into the birth and ministry of Jesus. We contemplate how we can follow Jesus as we contemplate his life, how our life can be inspired by his. Sometimes people making a retreat may be choosing a state of life, whether it be the single life, married life, or religious life, or other ways to live. Whatever it is, there are ways of choosing that Ignatius gives us. For people who have already chosen a state of life, it is good to contemplate in this week how we can strengthen our commitment to the life we have chosen. The third week, we focus on the passion and death of Jesus and what he suffered for us. Are we willing to suffer with him? The fourth week is about the resurrection and begins by meditating on Jesus appearing to Mary and the apostles. He ends with a beautiful contemplation on the love of God, which is where the exercises have been leading us. We hopefully come to the freedom of seeing we, too, are beloved children of God. Remember that Ignatius does not necessarily mean four weeks of seven days each. Some weeks might be longer than seven days, some might be shorter, and that is where the director can be a great help to us. The four weeks are meant to form us as Intentional Disciples, even though it would take the Church several hundred years to develop that catch phrase.

Annotation 5 is very simple. We should begin these exercises with an openness to what will be given to us by God, with a generous attitude, ready to give what might be asked. We also need courage to act on what might be asked of us. Remember that one enters these exercises with the intention of meeting God. If I go to a Tim Hortons drive thru, I know what to expect. I will be asked to pay for the coffee, and I will be given a coffee. Not much preparation is needed. If Pope Francis called saying he had something to ask of me and something to give me, I would do more preparation for that meeting. In the exercises we are not going to get a donut or

The Spiritual Exercises

meet the Pope; we are hoping to meet God. That is why we need to do it with openness, courage, and generosity.

Annotation 6 deals with a situation that often happens to the retreatant. As we go through the exercises, even though we are praying and meditating on the life of Jesus and the mysteries of God, sometimes the prayer appears dry. If that happens, and if we meet with the director the next day and say that nothing is happening and that we wonder if we should be praying about something else, the director will probably want to explore why this reading seems so dry to us. Could it be that the times we are praying or the way we are praying need to change to help us get more out of the readings? Could it be that something in our history is blocking us from hearing what the scripture is trying to tell us? When the Word of God doesn't seem alive, the director can be our biggest help.

Annotation 7 is where Ignatius brings up temptation. There is an old saying that in times of great grace we often face great temptations by the enemy of humankind, how Ignatius refers to the devil. Think of couples who are sometimes plagued by doubts days before their marriage. As we come closer to God on retreat, we may also be tempted. The director will remind you that God is present even in these times of temptation, and God will assist us, but here we need the openness, generosity, and courage the most. Annotation 8 deals with the concepts of consolation and desolation, and Ignatius points this out, but when this happens, the director will help to guide the retreatant through these experiences. These are very technical terms for Ignatius. Books have been written just about the meaning of desolation and consolation in the exercises. This is another place the retreatant will find the director extremely helpful.

Annotation 9 deals with how there are some things that are appropriate for the beginning of the retreat in week one, and some instructions should only be given in week two. If you think about this, it is quite natural. If someone is beginning to learn music, they start by learning the notes, maybe the C major scale, some simple chords from that scale, but there's no sense talking at the first lesson about different modes and majors and minors. That will come, but first the student should learn the basics and then move on to more advanced studies. It is the same with the spiritual life. We do things differently depending on where we are at in our relationship with God.

Annotation 10 takes up the same theme in a bit more detail. God calls people to these intense exercises to strengthen our faith, but the enemy of humanity does not want that to happen. In the first week, as the journey is starting, the temptations will be despair and discouragement. Ignatius gives the director a series of helpful insights to deal with discouragement and the fear that one will not be able to complete the exercises. These rules of discernment are especially applicable in the first week. In the second week, we may be tempted in other ways—to take on too much too quickly and want to become a great missionary or a great spiritual warrior. Here again the director will help the retreatant to get through these temptations. One of the real strokes of genius for Ignatius was to see that one needs a different set of rules as one progresses in the journey, and it is good to not get to the second week rules before the first week is finished.

The Spiritual Exercises

Annotation 11 is a reminder to the director not to go into details about what is to come in the exercises during week one. Week one is the foundation to what the rest of the exercises will become. It is important for the retreatant to really do the work of the first week before moving on. When I was young, I got a guitar and started to learn how to play. I wanted to learn how to play some songs quickly and did not really study too much basic stuff about the guitar. It was only many years later that I learned that one of the things that kept me back was that I did not know some of the basics about how to hold it, what to do with my hands, and basic music theory that really make playing guitar much more enjoyable. In the same way, Ignatius wants the retreatant to know in week one who they are in their relationship with God, and to face the places where they need to change. Future weeks are when one might see what changes can be done, but the work of week one, as hard as it can be at times, needs to be done first.

Annotation 12 deals with the timing of the exercises. Ignatius recommends each exercise be done in five one-hour periods each day, with repetitions of the readings during that time. He also warns against the temptation to cut the hour short, and if one is tempted to do that it might be a good discipline to add four or five minutes to the hour rather than reduce any of the time from it. There is a wisdom in this. I know personally I have often found that I did not get the deepest message from any one exercise the first or second time through, or even the third time. It is the same even with physical exercise—sometimes the repetitions are what get the best results.

In Annotation 13, Ignatius deals with the fact that some of the Spiritual Exercises might bring us great peace. He reminds us that we are not to stay longer than the hour because we like the feeling. We are not doing these exercises for the sake of the warm comfort that they sometimes bring, but we are doing these exercises to meet our God. Ignatius also warns that sometimes a prayer can seem dry. Here he encourages us to be faithful to the hour we committed to. We are not to cut it short when it feels hard. It is beneficial in keeping faithful to our commitment. Even in relationships with others, when we make a commitment to do something, even if it is not all that thrilling, we follow through with the commitment. How much more should we do that with God? If we offer him an hour, we should give him the full hour.

In Annotation 14, Ignatius urges prudence and wisdom. If we are faithful to the exercises, we will have our love of God and desire to follow God roused deeply at times. We will feel called to certain actions and choices, and many will be virtuous. Here the director should help the retreatant be realistic in discerning where we might follow God. We should consider what gifts God has given us. I had a friend who was a great priest, but during part of his formation, he discerned that when the choir was practising, he was called to do chores in the barn. The choir head agreed. Not everyone is called to evangelize in the Sahara. Some are. There is an adage that God does not call the qualified but qualifies the called. And it is true God will give the graces needed to those called to various ministries. When I was young, I thought I would play for the Chicago Blackhawks. A noble and lofty ambition, but not one God had given me the talent needed to

The Spiritual Exercises

achieve. Ignatius wants us to work for the Greater Glory of God. We will not do that if we do something we do not have the talent for.

Annotation 15 is directed squarely at the director. During the exercises, the goal of the retreatant is to open themselves to the will of God. When the person is open there might be a temptation for the director to try and move the person in a certain direction. Ignatius is clear. In normal life, when people are living day to day, we can be free to try and influence another. But in the retreat, the director is to listen and support. God is working with the retreatant. Over thirty years ago, when I was learning this kind of prayer, I used the tools to come to a decision I had been struggling with. As I re-entered my life, I began to move in the direction God was calling me, and the decision was not from God. I went back to my director and said I was sure the decision was wrong, and he agreed. He said he did not think I had done a good discernment. I asked him why he had not told me that. He simply said that I was pretty determined so he let me explore it. He thought I would be back, but he let the decision be mine. I learned a lot about how God will keep faithful until we get it right.

Annotation 16 is related to the above as well as the principle and foundation. We are at times strongly attracted to a job or place and feel that we believe is needed for our peace and true joy. Ignatius reminds us that we should be giving Glory to God, not ourselves. In the example above, I was more wanting God to follow my will. And God wanted me to follow a different path to bring his Glory about. It can be hard, but if one finds oneself overly attached to a person, place, or thing, we should pray for freedom from the attachment and ask for the opposite. Twelve-step programs have many things from the Spiritual Exercise built in. Step one is admitting you are not in control of something (for example, drinking in A.A.). Step two is admitting there is a higher power than yourself that can help. And step three is asking for that higher power's intervention. Any inordinate desire we have—for marriage, the priesthood, a certain job, or anything else—Ignatius encourages us to seek freedom from so we can freely embrace God's will. There is deep wisdom in the phrase *Let go and let GOD.*

Annotation 18 points out that the director does not need to be a priest, but the retreatant should have the same type of honesty with the director as they would with a confessor. Withholding certain information or desires from the director might mean that that they cannot offer all the help you may need. If I went to my doctor and did not mention blood in my stools because I thought that was gross and did not want to talk about it, he may not come up with a diagnosis and treatment plan to deal with an illness. The more information you give your director, the greater the possibility they might be able to help you find God in the middle of the confusion of life. Kenny Rogers sang about how in a poker game, you should "know when to hold them, know when to fold them, know when to walk away, know when to run." A thirty-day retreat is a privileged time where you look at the cards God has given you, discuss what God is showing you with a director, discard some cards and draw new ones. But if you do not show your hand to the director, he cannot help you discover how to play.

The Spiritual Exercises

Annotation 18 deals with the fact that each person will do the exercises in a way suited to them. Especially the first time, we should have an experienced director to customize the exercises for us. Age, personality, and life circumstances all can affect which parts of the exercises could be beneficial, and a director may even see possible negative consequences for us in others. Most can benefit from what are called week one exercises, but the wise director may not take the retreatant much further if it seems the retreatant is not yet ready. Personal trainers have a large variety of exercises they can show clients. But it would be malpractice for them to put my seventy-two-year-old body through exercises designed for a twenty-five-year-old professional athlete. In the same way, they should challenge the young athlete much more than they would me. You should be open with your director about who you are and how you are experiencing the exercises. Then they can give you appropriate exercises to get you the maximum graces from your retreat.

Annotation 19 explains that the exercises were designed to develop an everyday spirituality and they can be spread out over a long period. If the retreatant can manage about ninety minutes a day with a weekly meeting with their director that could work. It would take much more than thirty days, but over about a year one would develop a good prayer routine. The exercises need to be modified a little, but it is a good way of doing the exercises. That was the way I did the exercises the first time. I suspect Ignatius and his companions did the exercises that way often. It was probably a few years before there were Jesuit retreat houses.

Annotation 20 describes the advantages of going on a thirty-day silent retreat. The separation from friends, family, and routines allows us to enter in a time of intense prayer, with five sessions a day and daily meetings with a director. That helps us focus more clearly on God. For some the silence could be very hard and they might be better to try shorter silent retreats first, maybe for a weekend and then for a week. I know I loved my thirty-day retreat and still try to do an annual eight-day silent retreat. The formal exercises can of course be done more than once in a lifetime, but the real gift is that they teach a way of prayer that can work on shorter annual retreats and can help our daily prayer.

I hope this brief review of his notes, mainly to spiritual directors giving a retreat, might give you a sense of the complex role that develops between a director and a retreatant. A director can be considered a companion on your journey with God, someone who has walked the path before and might be able to help you name what you see on your journey. The director's job is to become less and less important as the retreatant and God get more actively engaged in their relationship. A counsellor might try and direct us to see different things; a director wants us to see what God is showing us. A retreat is not therapy, but may heal our relationship with God. Ignatius had a simple goal, that people would meet God, glorify his name, and tell others about God's great love. The last step in the twelve-step program encourages the stepper to go and share their good news of recovery. If Ignatius met you after doing the exercises, he would not be interested in your money, your position, your health, or any of the other things we put so much energy into

The Spiritual Exercises

developing. He would want to know if his exercises made you a more Intentional Disciple of Jesus, if they taught you how you might live that role. If he heard you say yes, he would know his system was still working,

Many folks balk a little at the thought of a thirty-day silent retreat. First, it is not all silence; you would meet with your director every day for about thirty minutes, and most retreat houses schedule a day in the middle where folks can leave and do something outside the retreat house. Some might opt to stay in silence, but others enjoy a little break. Your voice does indeed get a little break, but the silence is a crucial factor and worth the effort. Cellphones helped science discover why. Turning off cellphones while driving and talking when praying can be useful. Most of us know how to ask things from God, and even how to praise and thank God. Ignatius reminds us that prayer also includes deep listening to God.

People began to be concerned about texting while driving. Statistics showed it was not a good idea, and the internet was encouraging many other kinds of multitasking. Psychologists, with the help of modern technologies, are beginning to understand how the brain works with brain imaging and behavioural experiments. They concluded that not only texting and driving but all multitasking reduced performance. The reason was simple. All decisions happen in one place in the brain, and if you multitask, you must keep switching from one task to another. One advantage of working at home during COVID was that people found their productivity increased due to less interactions with bosses and co-workers. Parents of infants did not see the benefits quite as much. We work better and focus more when we keep our focus on one thing.

That is why people love the exercises. You reduce distractions and for five hours a day for four weeks focus on God. No email, phone, and such. It is something Ignatius knew five hundred years ago, long before cellphones. And that is why he preferred Annotation 20 over 19, but both can work. It is harder to get off the grid for ninety minutes a day for a year, but it can be done.

Ignatius ends his notes by stressing again that the exercises are meant to free the retreatant from disordered attachments so that they can freely go where God asks. In the early days of the Jesuits, the members kept a packed bag in their room so they could leave at once when and if they were asked. I am not a Jesuit, and I am not sure if any still do that. He also stresses that the director and retreatant need to respect each other to get maximum benefit. This sometimes means letting go of our beliefs and practices, even some treasured ones. It is amazing how many different things might be gleaned from a few lines of scripture when meditated on for many hours. The purpose is not Bible study as such, but to discover if God might use the passage to communicate a message to the retreatant. The retreatant and director should trust each other and not get into theological debates. The retreat may not settle in your mind whether God parted the waters of the Red Sea for Moses, but it may help you discover in the story obstacles God has cleared for you, or that you need cleared in your life.

Now to week one, which starts with the Principle and Foundation.

The Spiritual Exercises

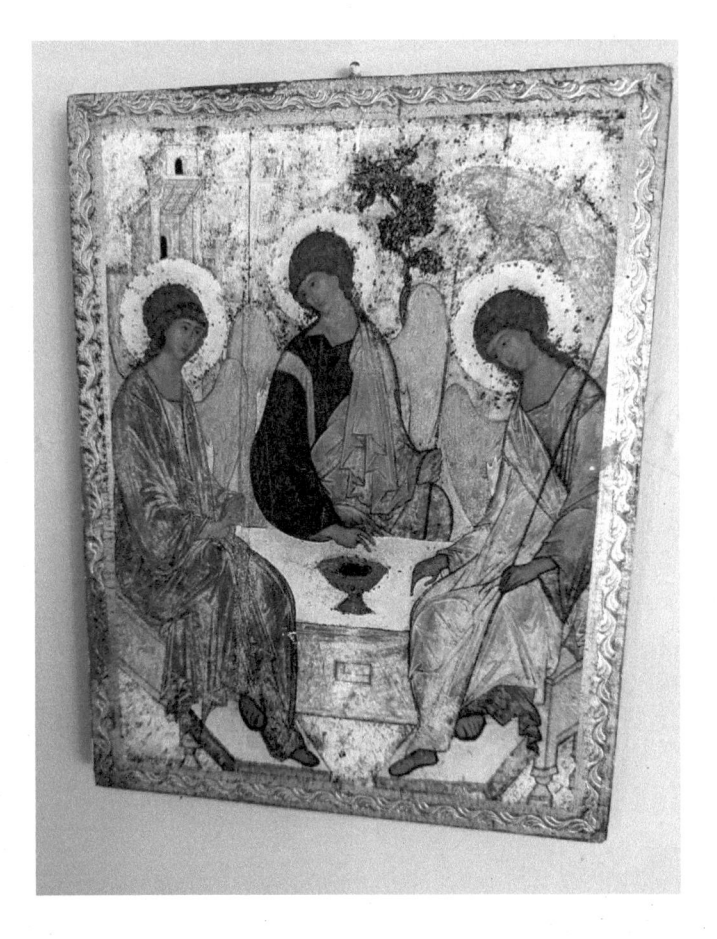

There is a theory about the little square at the bottom that has dried glue on it. Some speculate that Rublev, in a stroke of inspiration, might have inserted a small mirror there, so the viewer could see themselves seated between the Father and the Spirit across from the Son at the table. Whether that was the intent of Rublev or not, it is certainly what Ignatius hoped for those doing his exercises—that they would enter into a deep, intimate conversation with God.

The First Week

Getting Started: The Principle and Foundation

When you start the Spiritual Exercises, you begin with week one. As mentioned previously, the term *week* is very loose. Especially for someone new to this sort of prayer, week one can be extended by the director quite a bit, and as mentioned, the exercises for this week might be all some folks are ready to do at the time. Even for people who do week one in about one week or less, the director has latitude, and not everyone does the same exercises, in the same order. This should not be surprising. Even with physical exercises with a personal trainer, a personal program is developed to best meet the needs of each client. Therefore, it is important to work with a director and not just pick up a book describing the exercises. Once you have been through the exercises, a book describing the exercises might be useful, but think of it as lecture notes to review. Do not use it as a self-help book before you know what it describes. I will not be describing too many specific exercises as I go through this book, mainly because if you do the exercises one day, you may do different things. As you do the exercises, your director might see some of the additional exercises as being more suitable for you.

Having said all that, every retreatant will start with the Principle and Foundation. Again, David L. Fleming, SJ, in *Draw Me into Your Friendship* has a beautiful contemporary translation, but in this case, I prefer the bare bones literal translation he also includes:

> "Man is created to praise, reverence, and serve God or Lord and by this means to save his soul.
>
> "And the other things on the face of the earth are created for man and that they may be help him in prosecuting the end for which he is created. From this it follows that man is to use them as much as they help him on to his end, and ought to rid himself of them so far as they hindered him as to it.
>
> "For this it is necessary to make ourselves indifferent to all created things in all that is allowed to the choice of our free will and is not prohibited to it; so that, on our part, we want not health rather than sickness, riches rather than poverty, honor rather than dishonor, long rather than short life, and so in all the rest; desiring and choosing only what is most conducive for us to the end for which we are created." [3]

The Spiritual Exercises

Now I apologize for the non-inclusive language and grammar that my mother the English teacher would not approve of. The key is found in the first line. We are created to praise, reverence, and *serve* God. This concept usually shows up early in catechisms. That is how we will save our souls. And saving our souls is another way of saying getting to spend eternity in a loving relationship with God. The praising and reverencing are not done because God needs our praise and reverence. The God who brought the universe into existence in a powerful act of creative love 13 billion years ago does not need me to say good job, well done. But I need to deepen my awareness of this being who is more than I can even imagine, and my praise and reverence need to find fulfilment in serving God by being a good steward of the gifts I have been given. I need to develop a certain indifference to creation, not disdain, and acceptance of where I am as I realize that I was made by God for heaven, not to create heaven on earth. An old spiritual summarizes it well: "Keep your eye on the prize, hold on." The Principle and Foundation is holding on and using what brings us to God and letting go of what I do not need for that task. And the exercises can help us know how to achieve that.

As a retreatant starts the journey, the director will encourage them to pray with these words a few times a day. They may suggest a scripture passages to reflect on with them; Ignatius recommended thirteen possibilities, but there could be more. The Principle and Foundation is deeply rooted in biblical themes. If you want to play chess, it is good to know you are trying to checkmate your opponent. To play an instrument, it is good to know the type of music you want to play so you choose the right instrument and scales and modes. In hockey, you need to know on which goal to score and which one to avoid scoring on. Ignatius wants to help you get to heaven, and the Principle and Foundation is where you start.

Facing Our Sins

The goal of week one is to come to see ourselves honestly. This means we need to first see that we are created beings and we have a creator. We need to see where we lived in accord with our creator, and where we followed the advice of Frank Sinatra and "did it our way." In theological terms, we need to be honest about the virtues we possess and the vices we practice. Now Ignatius is wise in asking us to always start such an analysis by expressing gratitude to God and asking God to help us to see in truth our strengths and weaknesses. This is important. If we just try to see our faults and do not see them in the context of a life graced by God, where we have at times not always responded with love to the Love God has for us, we can feel despair. We can be too hard on ourselves. I have found in the past when I have asked employees to do a self-evaluation that around 90 per cent of the time I have them upgrade their opinions.

But in truth, apart from Jesus and Mary, all of us have areas where we sin some of the time. And while these areas do not mean we can never have a close relationship with God, Ignatius knew that our sins needed our attention before we could have true intimacy with God. Even in our human-to-human relationships we need to be honest, and if we make mistakes, admit them and try to make amends for any harm we may have done. As a priest, I have too often seen rifts in families and friendships that can be traced to some unreconciled conflict. As I write this, there are even some situations like that in the British royal family. Ignatius wisely asks us in week one to be honest with ourselves in how we have lived our relationship with God. For many it is the hardest week, but in the end, we find that the freedom of being open with ourselves, and with God is the most liberating part of the exercises.

The A.A. Experience: The Start of Change

I mentioned earlier that the two men who founded Alcoholics Anonymous modelled part of their program on the Spiritual Exercises. They had the help of a Jesuit as they were forming their Twelve Step Program. In many ways, The first ten steps were heavily influenced by the work that Ignatius asks retreatants to do in week one. And it is the people who internalize these steps that experience the freedom of having their higher power free them from their addiction. Some of weeks two and three work might happen in step eleven, although for a non-Christian, this would be lived differently than Ignatius envisioned. And the healing and freedom Ignatius brings us to in week four is what step twelve is all about, although, again, a non-Christian would have a different approach. I mention this just to point out that the twelve-step programs that have healed many people of serious addictions centre around concepts found in the exercises, especially week one.

The twelve steps were designed for people of any or no faith, so there is no attempt to understand or name the higher power. Being a Catholic, Ignatius had no trouble naming the Trinity as the higher power, and he designed his exercises to help one experience God's love and mercy. The first week is sometimes referred to as sin week. It is in many ways an appropriate name. The Catholic Church is often accused of focusing too much on sin. But when one understands what Ignatius is doing in this week, we see he is only bringing us to see our sinfulness so that we can free ourselves from it and move into the relationship God desires to have with us. Over the past ten years or so, I have tried to improve in a couple of activities I had participated in for forty to fifty years. I had played guitar from my early teens and golf from my mid-twenties, although I had caddied during the summer in high school.

For golf improvement I found a golf professional who was a teaching pro. She suggested adjustments that I could make to my game and approach to playing, but not right away. First, she had to address several bad habits I had developed around how I placed my hands on the club, how I positioned my feet as I stood over the ball, how I shifted my weight during the swing, and such. These bad habits were my golfing sins, and until I gave them up, I would never be able to focus on playing golf or feel the joy of watching the golf ball do what I desired. I had to break the bad habits and develop new ones.

With the guitar playing, I started learning songs, basic strumming patterns, and the basic open string chords sometimes called cowboy chords. I never learned theory, or scales, never knew why the chords were what they were. I knew for some chords you could strum all six strings, some you should only strum five, and the poor D chord should only get four strings strummed, although I did not know why. Although there were over twenty frets on the guitar with well over one hundred and twenty places where you could play individual notes, I almost stayed exclusively in the first five frets, and if someone had taken the rest out, I would not have missed them. When I started to learn about scales, modes, chord theory, and soloing, the rest of the guitar neck opened up for me. But I found here as well I had picked up bad habits about hand position, how I held the guitar, picking individual notes, and muting some strings. I needed new habits. Just as I had developed golfing sins, I had guitar sins I needed to work on.

I could go on. When I retired and started to do my own cooking, I had to develop new skills or get a part-time job to pay for eating out all the time. Anytime we want to develop something new that we desire, it often involves breaking an old habit and developing a new one. It is the same with new relationships. One of my grandfathers was a decorated Marine, but my grandmother was not going to marry someone in the military, so he drove streetcars in Boston. In the Church we describe bad habits as sins and good habits as virtues. Modern day psychology will tell you that most of what we do is done unconsciously and is habitual. I had to consciously focus on how to hold my hands and other things to change my golf game and guitar playing. I needed to replace the habits that were hindering me with ones that would allow me to do what I desired. Ignatius knew that if we want to live with a deeper awareness of God's love and plan for us, we need to change sinful habits into virtues. That is why he starts with sin week.

The Examen

Now, looking at our sins is not something we enjoy, but I think most see the benefit of overcoming a bad habit. An alcoholic in recovery for twenty-five years may tell you how sobriety seemed impossible twenty-six years ago, but they are grateful for each current day without a drink. The temptations in this week will often be quite different than what one will face later in the exercises. A good director will help with facing them. Ignatius encourages looking at the reality of sin: early stories of angels rebelling, our first ancestors committing original sin, and our personal sins as well. But Ignatius never forgets the Principle and Foundation, how we were made to love, honour, and serve God, and that our sins and bad habits are keeping us from that purpose. Ignatius wants us to pray for the grace to have sorrow for our sins. He also wants us to face the possibility of failing and ending up in hell, not heaven. The purpose of sin week is not only to know our sins but to feel the shame and sorrow we should have for them so that we can bring them out of the unconscious realm, focus on them clearly, choose to seek virtue over vice, and abandon the behaviours that are harming others and ourselves.

To help us, Ignatius also recommends examining our consciences at noon and in the evening. He always starts with looking at the graces we received. If we are not aware of God's gifts and just look at our faults, we are missing the point. Again, modern psychologists would agree with Ignatius here, and one thing they would advise to combat depression is listing the things for which you are grateful. A saying you will often hear from twelve steppers is that one should develop an attitude of gratitude. We often tell each other to count our blessings. Ignatius's good advice for breaking a habit is to list how many times we do it in each hour. Most people find that simply listing how often we do something reduces the frequency. Again, modern psychology would agree with Ignatius, that listing moves the behaviour from an unconscious act to our conscious mind, where we can decrease it.

Let me give one simple example of applying this. I gained weight during COVID. Looking at my life, I realized that I had been buying cookies as snacks and often getting coffee and a donut when driving. Now eating a cookie or a donut is not a great sin, but as I started to track the frequency, I saw a habit had developed that was taking it into excess. Just being aware reduced the problem a little, but I also needed to consciously decide to change the snacks. I bought fruit to snack on and consciously told myself when I got in the car not to pull into a Tim Hortons drive thru. Changing the habits is helped to reduce some of the weight. Doing something about my "sin" stopped it from being something I felt bad about, and breaking the habit gave me something to be grateful for. Net result: facing the "sin" and acting to change brought me to a better place to relate with God. Ignatius wants us to see our sins and have deep remorse for them, not so we can take antidepressants, but so we can see how God will bring us to a place where we are free of them.

A truth we all learn as we age is that we will change. My siblings and I have changed our relationships over the years. It has been close to sixty-five years since I even thought of placing a garter snake in my sister's boots. Sometimes after a celebration we see the mess that needs cleaning up. But we do the dishes and mop the floor and we feel good, and we can remember with gratitude the celebration we had and let go of the dirty dishes. In week one, Ignatius wants us to see the dirty dishes and start scrubbing. Now a sink full of dishes is obvious, but we are often led away from virtue by more subtle means. It can even be one cookie at a time over months. In A.A. the language used to describe what Ignatius is getting at is "hitting bottom."

Confession: Healing Our Souls

An alcoholic in recovery has learned they need to quit drinking to gain recovery. Only then can they see the harm their drinking is causing themselves and others. Then they can ask for help from their higher power. They can make a moral inventory, see what is working in their life as well as the harm they have done to themselves and others. They then give it away, share their inventory with another. The language Ignatius uses is a general examination of consciousness, a look at one's life, seeing where God has graced us, and seeing where we have let bad habits separate us from God and others, and even lowered our own self-esteem. There should be no fudging. There might have been circumstances that led us astray but admit the harm. Often a Catholic might seek out a priest to make a general confession. Even non-Catholic alcoholics sometimes seek a priest to give their moral inventory away to. They may not be ready to go to confession and join the church, but they know priests have heard a lot, and sometimes alcoholics have done a lot.

A brief note on confession. The priest may hear the sins confessed and suggest a penance or even an act to amend for a harm, but confession is not about being judged for your crimes—it is seeking God's healing of places of hurt in your life. When one goes to confession, it is not going to court. It is more like going to the doctor and asking for healing. We tell our doctors our symptoms and hope he can help us alleviate them. Our doctor diagnoses the issue, recommends a course of action, but trusts us to act on it. A relative recently got a new knee. Her surgeon told her she would get the knee she wants. He meant he had changed the knee, but it was up to her to do the physio and care for the new knee if she wanted it to work. He knew the old one was not ever going to do the job. She now had a new knee, but she had to use it well. Having had two knees replaced, I can attest to his advice. It is the same with confession. We go to the divine healer through the priest. He absolves us, gives us a fresh start, but unless we change our habits, the sins will return.

Ignatius invites us to start the exercises by facing our sins, the habits we have that harm ourselves and others and that keep us from knowing God's love. I often tell people that sometimes we go to a family gathering and there might be something we have done to another family member. If we do not apologize before the meal starts, the "sin" will be the elephant in the room for the whole meal. If we make our amends before the meal, the gathering will be much more enjoyable. Ignatius knows we can meet God in a more intense way during these exercises. He leads us to clear up any habits that might be keeping us from experiencing God's love. What Ignatius knew was that all of us know we are sinners. We cannot change the past. We may have sinned, but he wants us to begin this new more intense relationship with God—not as sinners, but as forgiven sinners and beloved children of God. In the language of A.A., we become recovering sinners.

Week one is sin week but may better be called "letting go of sin" week. In A.A. they say after we have given away our inventory that step six is being ready to let God remove all our defects of character, and step seven is humbly asking God to remove our shortcomings. Now sometimes people who were seriously addicted have done things for which they need to make amends. Sometimes we have dealt with such serious sins long before we feel called to the exercises, but various twelve-step programs might be helpful in some circumstances. But we might be struggling with resentment, anger, jealousy, or other character traits that we should address before we begin week two. For many, this week is not a long struggle, and it may be only a few days before our director moves us on. Habits, like a daily examens, might even be started before the retreat and are good to continue after. Early on we will often be tempted to believe we will never be able to change, feeling our habits will always be there. Then God heals us, and we begin to see his power when we let him in, and we realize God loves us. Then we are ready for week two.

During the first week, you will be given broad guidelines for prayer. Ignatius recommends five-hour periods, or for some people four. You will be given a focused idea or short Gospel passage to meditate on. You will often use this for all five hours. Stay with the hour. Sometimes you will be tempted to stop sooner. Finish the hour. Sometimes you might want to stay longer. Finish at the hour. After each hour, you will be invited to discuss your prayer experience briefly, first with Mary, next with Jesus, and lastly with the Father.

The Spiritual Exercises

These triple colloquies are not long but are important. Many also find a short journal entry is helpful. Maybe keep your journal by your bed, as your dreams might be interesting, and if we do not write them down, we will forget them.

The prayer discipline may seem a bit obsessive at first, but it does work. If you were doing weight training, your trainer would tell you how much weight to use for each exercise and how many reps to do. Then your body needs recovery. If you do too many reps, you may need a much longer recovery, and if you do too few, you may not strain enough to build up muscles. The repetitions often move the meditation from the head to the heart, and I often found repetition five far deeper and more meaningful than my first meditation. It is the same with weights. You may start with ten pounds, but slowly you find you can lift more.

One last instruction you will get in week one is to stay focused on the short meditations you are given. You will not be asked to meditate on chapters 5 to 7 in Matthew, the Sermon on the Mount. You may be asked to meditate on a few verses of it. The Spiritual Exercises will get you to look at several crucial parts of the life of Christ. They are not a biblical study; Ignatius wants you to meet the risen Jesus, to know how much you are loved by God and choose to follow. If you take the journey he advises and keep faithful, you will encounter God in a new way, and hopefully choose to follow God. You will find the scriptures come alive in a new way. You may find yourself loving more, being more tolerant and less frustrated about things. And you will know you are loved unconditionally. Surely that might be worth a few days to let God remove our shortcomings.

Hints For Living Week One

It is worth considering how Ignatius plans the week to go. There are to be five distinct prayer periods of an hour apiece. The first two will have a short scripture passage assigned to each of them. For period three, you would repeat the meditation on hour one; for period four, you would repeat the meditation for period two. The fifth hour is where Ignatius gets specific. He wants you to vividly imagine the scene. If you are in the manger, who might be there, what animals, is it darkly lit, what smells are there. This was the hardest thing for me to learn, because even in daily life I am not often that aware of my physical surroundings. But by vividly focusing on what the scene was like, there is more chance of our emotions getting involved. In our brains we have a small area at the front that processes written words, a small area at the back that processes words we hear, and a large area where we sort and categorize our thoughts to experience how we feel about them. For the final hour, Ignatius wants us to experience how the passages affect our emotions. Why will become apparent in the second week.

People often speak about how the longest journey we make in life is from the head to the heart. Modern MRI research into the brain shows that while we have data collection points for sight, sound, smell, touch, and taste, they all get thrown into a part of the brain where their emotional content is rated, and decisions are made. We taste a food, but we need to know if we like the taste or not. Ignatius calls this final prayer period the application of the senses. We have heard that God became man in the person of Jesus. Ignatius asks us to see how we would feel if we saw Mary, a young girl

The Spiritual Exercises

holding her child; how we would feel watching God assuming the vulnerability of a newborn; how Joseph felt.

By applying our senses to vividly imagine distinct parts of the story, over the course of the retreat Ignatius will be inviting us to not only recall that God became man, suffered and died for us, rose from the dead, and will come again. He also wants us to truly face how we feel about Jesus, how we have responded to God in the past, and how we will in the future. Can we get away from knowing about Jesus to loving Jesus, and can we accept his love and discover our response to being loved by God? We may be attracted to another, but we do not marry and share our lives with another because we like them. But we do if we love them. Jesus asked Peter in John's Gospel if Peter loved him. Ignatius wants to bring us with his exercises to say to Jesus that we love him and will make him our ultimate purpose. Peter was told to feed his sheep. Jesus also has a task for us.

Ignatius does have two helpful suggestions that can help us with our prayer. The first is simple. Before you retire for the night, take a moment to consider the passages you will be praying with the next day; ask God to bless your prayers the next day. Very brief. And when you wake the next day, do not let your mind wander. Focus on what you will be praying about that day and ask again for your prayer to be blest. These are two graced moments, where we work on focusing on our desire to know, love, and serve God throughout the whole day. It is a bit easier at a retreat house if we are off the grid to remember to give the day to God. As you enter the silence, you will become aware that God is present in moments in between the formal prayer periods.

While we hopefully grow in our awareness of God's presence in all our life, Ignatius has a suggestion of somehow acknowledging re-entering into his presence before each period of prayer. It should be a brief greeting; Ignatius says no longer than the time it would take to say an Our Father. I know when I was a child, most people blest themselves when they entered church and genuflected before taking their seat. But Ignatius wants us not to just acknowledge God but try to see how he looks on us. When I was a child, my father took a train from the city to our town and walked twenty minutes to our house, and he and my mother always greeted each other when he arrived. The short ritual let them both know that the brief separation of the day was over, they were back together in person. They had been in each other's minds and hearts, but now they were present to each other again. That is what Ignatius hopes will develop in our relationship with God.

While Ignatius is fussy about many other things, he is free about our stance while praying. We are all different, and different meditations may suggest distinct positions. He only says we should be relaxed and at ease. Our position should not distract but foster our prayer. You are free to stand, sit, kneel, or lie down. Whatever works is good. If your prayers are bringing sorrow or remorse you may wish to kneel. If your meditation is making you aware of the majesty of God, you may wish to stand. You may want to sit with God. You might lie under the stars with God, who made them. His only cautions are if your stance is working during a meditation, stick with it. A leisurely stroll may bring you close to God, a power walk or run not as likely to have that effect.

The Spiritual Exercises

There may be someone out there who could be at ease with God while supporting themselves balanced on one hand for an hour, but I doubt it. Find what works for that day. And let that be your stance.

After the prayer is over, Ignatius recommends a review be made for about fifteen minutes. The review is not to be made of any brilliant theological insights we might have had. It is more to reflect on the movements we experienced in the prayer. Were there moments of consolation or desolation? Were there moments we struggled with distractions? Were we sometimes fearful or anxious, did feelings persist, were they disturbing? Maybe if we were praying about the nativity, we may have seen Jesus looking at us with big brown eyes. Not important. If we felt loved and cared for in his gaze, take note. Journal some of these emotional moments, as they will become how we experience God directly as the retreat progresses. Thank God for graces received, and if we were praying for a particular grace, note if it was received, and if not, try and understand if we were resisting.

It is helpful to choose the proper environment in which we should pray. During the first week, with its focus on sin, we should seek quiet places, even dimly lit places, where we will not be distracted. We will be tempted to focus on anything else at times. Maybe even remember a joke to shift our focus. Keep focused and find a place where that will be possible. Most young children when they are caught misbehaving by their parents have trouble looking their parents directly in the eye and admitting their fault. Their eyes dart here and there looking for relief. They attempt to change the subject, shift the blame, rationalize the behaviour. But a loving parent keeps drawing their focus back until they can face their fault. The parent knows that it is only then that they can resolve to change. During the first week, we will be tempted to use those tactics we used as a child. Do not do it. Keep your eyes on the truth of who you are. In that moment of truth, God can heal you. As mentioned, in A.A. they call it hitting bottom. The first week invites us to hit bottom, but only so we can experience God picking us up, and over the other weeks grow in our relationship with God and experience the height of human experience, living as a beloved child of God.

One difficult conversation one might have with the director is penance. Now today in the Catholic Church, one refers to the sacrament where one confesses one's sins to a priest as the Sacrament of Reconciliation. The formal name is the Rite of Penance but is often just called confession. Confessing, admitting of sins, is a part of the process. Today the emphasis is hopefully on reconciling and renewing the relationship with God. The 1970s movie *Love Story* included a silly catchphrase: "Love means never having to say you're sorry." Truth be told, after over seventy years on this planet, I would say love means always having to say you are sorry, and that has been very true about my relationship with God. And the first week will make us aware of sins that need healing, and whether it is to a priest sacramentally or a lay director, we will have to give our confession away, just as in A.A. people give their Fearless Moral Inventory away. The old saying is true: confession is good for the soul.

The trickiest part of the entire process is our penance. Ignatius knew this and explained that there was inner and exterior penance. Now by far the most straightforward is

The Spiritual Exercises

interior penance where, in our own minds, we feel sorrow or contrition for our sins and resolve to try to avoid them in the future. In the Catholic Church, we begin all our services with a form of act of contrition to reconcile ourselves to God as we come together. We believe that minor sins we mentally bring to God are forgiven at this time, although serious sins should be dealt with in formal reconciliation. I know few who have strong objections to this process of interior penance. Many Christian traditions believe that that is the way to go, and their confession is personally confessing to God, not a minister.

Exterior penances can be more of a problem, and Ignatius in his own life sometimes went overboard at times, so he says to talk to your director before beginning any. In the history of the Church some have slept on nails, whipped themselves, and done various other things. It is important to not harm oneself with a penance. We can reduce food, or a kind of food, but not to the point it would harm us. We may sleep less sometimes, maybe stay up for a vigil, but for best mental health, you should average seven to eight hours of sleep. Bodily penances should not harm the body or wound us. All penances should be done out of love and not as a punishment or as a bargaining chip with God.

The A.A. program speaks of making amends, not penance. This is a healthy stance. Trying to make amends for harm done might involve making sacrifices. Sometimes it involves doing something to try and make up for our harmful actions. I know of drunk drivers who have done great damage but who spent years talking to groups, especially youth, to try and dissuade them from drinking and driving. When I engaged in prison ministry, I met a man who was a former gang member. He visited many prisons. His aim was not high. He told me if he could turn around one young guy a year, he could prevent great suffering they might have caused. That was his penance. Penances like this are done out of love. People hoped that their actions would bring others to experience God's healing love. Following God might at times cause us pain, even martyrdom in rare cases. Ignatius would say those sufferings could be offered to God, but he would not suggest one should seek out harm to ourselves and death.

External penances first help us bring our bodies in line with our wills to follow God. When I wanted to improve my guitar and golf, I had to resolve to learn, of course, but I also had to get my body doing what I had resolved to do. Our brain learns from what our body learns. Our souls are united with our bodies, and external penances can bring our body where our soul wants to be. Saying "I am sorry I spilt the milk" is nice. Cleaning up the mess shows others and myself that I want to repair some of the consequences. We cannot put the milk back in the glass, but we should do what we can to improve the situation.

I knew a recovering alcoholic who was healed by God's love. He returned to practicing his faith but felt a call to assume a new task. He became a volunteer at a hospital, where he began to drive patients to chemotherapy treatments. This external act not only helped others, but it also reminded him that he had received a great healing, and he in a small way available to him was helping others to heal. All our penances should be grateful responses to graces received, not negotiation with God. Remember the Principle and

The Spiritual Exercises

Foundation. We were made to praise, reverence, and serve God. God was not created to reward us for the small tasks we do. Our daily examens can help us keep track of how we are doing with our prayer.

A lot goes on in the first week. We are learning a new way to pray. We are focusing more on how we feel than what we think. We hopefully have learned how God is always present to us and faced the areas in our life where we have not been present to God. Depending on our relationship with God when we begin the exercises, the first week may be shorter or longer than seven days. None of that matters in the end. When you have done the work, your director will begin the exercises in the second week. Here the exercises really begin to come alive.

Second Week

The second week of the exercises is again flexible in length and passages covered. For many folks who do the exercises, the goals of the first week will be accomplished quickly, especially if one is making a thirty-day retreat. That is because very few jump into a thirty-day silent retreat unless they have been familiar with prayer for a while, and they have come to a point where they are more interested in the aids in discernment, possibly because of upcoming life decisions. And while they might be quite comfortable with a refresher of first-week topics, the second week is when the exercises become more pointed.

Ignatius starts the week with images of his day. He asks the retreatant to imagine a great king, one who is just, who wishes to bring belief to the world. This ruler brings equity to his people, listens to their hopes and dreams, and tries to meet them. Ignatius asks us to imagine how easy it would be for us to offer our allegiance to this king, even to the point of going to battle for him and even losing our life for such a virtuous ruler. For the second half of the meditation, Ignatius asks us to imagine Christ as the king. To pledge our loyalty and lives to following Christ who desires so much good for his people.

It is good to remember that Christ can be thought of as a king. His subjects follow him, and those that do not follow, who stop being subjects, find someone or something else to follow, but they are always welcome back. The Gold Coast, now part of Ghana, was where most African slaves were sent off to the Caribbean, the United States, and other places. It was a shameful period in history, enabled by colonialism. Many died in the ships, and if they survived, they and their descendants suffered much brutality. It was not humanity's finest hour and could be in the running for one of our worst hours. But I recently learned that any descendants of those sent off to be slaves can obtain Ghanian citizenship. In the same way, Christ welcomes all who choose to follow him to find a place in his kingdom. Those of us in organized religions have courses and rituals to join our churches. Christ just wants people to come and follow.

While Ignatius usually recommends doing an exercise five or at least four times in a day, at the start of week two, he says do this exercise twice, once on rising and once around the evening meal. He recommends doing spiritual reading like the lives of the saints or scripture, but not the Gospels. This is another place where Ignatius was quite brilliant. During week one exercises, retreatants deal with serious issues. Ignatius says relax a bit as we begin to come into a closer relationship with Jesus. Play with the idea of having him as our sovereign we love and follow. He does not want you reading the Gospels because he is going to take you to specific places and does not want you jumping ahead. In his day books were not common. When he was recuperating from battle injuries he had two books he could read, either The Bible or The Lives of the Saints. In the past he had found the romantic novels he had read stirred his imagination, but they did not stay with him. The stories of Jesus and the saints however stayed in his imagination for days, inspiring him to follow their examples. This was the start of his theory of consolation and desolation, a pivotal insight. That personal history might have influenced his reading suggestions.

The next day it is back to serious meditations on focused items. His first contemplation is the mystery of the incarnation. Next, he has us focus on the nativity. For the third hour we repeat the same material. For the fourth hour we get to repeat again. And for the final hour we repeat, but this time with attention focused on the five senses. What smells did we smell in the stable? Were there sounds, did Jesus cry, were there animals around, were they noisy? This kind of meditation is much easier for people who are sensitive to the sights and sounds around them every day. Often one will receive great insights when we let the Spirit into our imagination. Years ago, the Myers-Briggs test was popular. On it I was strong on the intuition scale, and weak on the sensate scale. What that means is if you ask me about someone, I might come close to telling you how they were feeling, but don't ask me what they were wearing or the colour of their hair or eyes. I found Ignatius asking me to apply my senses in the meditation difficult, but after years of trying, I can say it is worth it.

In this week, Ignatius calls us to sometimes alter the colloquies if desired. Maybe rather than three conversations for the incarnation, just talk to Mary. Or maybe we might want to have the three talks with the three persons of the Trinity. The important thing is to discuss the hour of prayer. He also stresses to remain conscious that you are on retreat and seeking the graces of coming into a more intimate relationship with Christ. He advises that as we rise, we remind ourselves of the mysteries that we are focusing on that day. He asks us to recollect ourselves before we pray, to remind ourselves we are coming before God. If you had five meetings a day with your boss, you would review why you were going there, and maybe try to sense how he accepts you. Ignatius says the time it would take to say an Our Father should do the trick. This is again an area where modern psychology agrees with Ignatius. If we take a moment to prepare ourselves before any encounter, we have a better chance of achieving our desired results.

Ignatius does recommend a schedule for the day to accommodate the five hours of prayer. He does admit that for some people, four might be better, and the times of the day can vary. The first prayer period he recommends should occur around midnight, or a couple of hours after you go to bed. This is not something a psychologist would endorse. There is a long history in the Church of people recommending sticking some prayer in between sleep periods. Modern studies with MRIs and such show that we have a rhythm of sleep where we go through distinct stages, and we finish each stage with REM sleep, or dreaming. If you can get eight hours a night (recommended for adults), you will have on average four of these cycles. Although no one knows exactly what the brain does during these eight hours, there is good evidence that it contributes to better mental health. While waking briefly to write down a dream or use the washroom seems OK, it might not be a good idea to interrupt your sleep every night for over an hour as you go to your place to pray, have your colloquies, and write in your journal. I suspect most would benefit more from getting eight hours of uninterrupted sleep and doing five prayer periods in their sixteen waking hours.

For the next day, the first hour might be the Presentation, the second the Flight into Egypt. Again, the third and fourth hours would be repeating these events, and for the last hour, an application of the senses to really imagine ourselves there, hearing, seeing, smelling, tasting, and touching everything in our mind. If the retreatant and their director opt for four prayer periods in the day, the adaptation should be to do the two meditations, and rather than two repetitions, just do one and keep the application of the senses.

The next day, we are asked to look a little at what has been called the hidden life of Jesus. Now, it was not so much hidden as just not talked about. Once you get to be my age, I suspect you have met hundreds, even thousands, of people. If you are anything like me, you know a little about them, but their childhood, size of family, where they went to school, and thousands of other details you do not know. Of the eighty-nine chapters in the four Gospels about Jesus, only four mention anything about before Jesus was baptized, and most of those chapters in Matthew and Luke are about his birth. Luke does give us a few short verses about the time between his birth and Flight into Egypt and his Baptism. Ignatius invites us to meditate for an hour on how Jesus was subject to his parents as he developed as a human, and another hour on his adventures in the temple at twelve. The two repetitions and the application of the senses are to follow as usual. This can be an important day because it is easier to connect with the humanity of Jesus when we see him being born and being raised by Mary and Joseph and as a young man learning his trade. Each year at Christmas, I love watching the children gather around the crib. A few hundred years before Ignatius, Francis knew we needed to know the human Jesus to appreciate the Divinity of Jesus, so he created the crèche.

Seeking Christian Aspirations

The next day, Ignatius gives us another fact to consider. By looking at Jesus's hidden life, we hopefully noticed that as he grew, he had to progress from total obedience to his parents to beginning to be about his Father's business. We too, if we wish to follow Jesus, must be willing to grow and make the priorities of God take precedence in our lives. This day the retreatant is invited to look at their own life, what type of person are they.

The first meditation of the day calls us to ponder the evils that exist in the world: the wars, the prejudices, hunger, homelessness, the list could go on. Ignatius posits the cause of the evil in a good world made by a good God is Lucifer (the light bearer) who spotlights wealth, pride, and honour with his light to distract from being good. Many dismiss any talk of the Devil. Even many who believe in a good God resist the idea of a malevolent being working to lead us away from God for evil purposes. The problem is if we deny the existence of the Devil, then we must admit that we are the source of evil,

The Spiritual Exercises

there are no noble savages, no possibility of humans creating utopias. If there is no Devil to overcome, if we are just destined by our genetic programs to choose wealth until it is just greed and let others suffer, we are doomed to lie and cheat and do whatever it takes to gain honour, even if it means dishonouring others. And the pride we feel if we achieve wealth and honour is a great good, just too bad there was only enough for me. As a teenager I laughed at Flip Wilson's tag line "The Devil made me do it." And Ignatius would agree; the Devil cannot make us do anything. But Ignatius would say he does work hard at tempting us to do things that make God's will for the world difficult to achieve. Lucifer has good marketers.

In the second part of this meditation, Ignatius asks us to consider the ways of Jesus. While Lucifer draws us with the lure of wealth, power, and status, Jesus calls us to share the Good News freely with the world. While Lucifer wants us to become attached to the things of this world, Jesus calls us to take the graces we receive from a loving God and be ready to let go of what we do not need. It is not that Jesus wants everyone sleeping in ditches at the side of the road and going through garbage looking for scraps of food. But he does ask us to take what we need and not always be looking for more. As a Catholic priest, I can get by on less than a father of ten children. I do not have to worry about feeding and housing twelve people, just myself. If we can be humble enough to see that all we have is a gift, we can grow in our gratitude for what we have and enjoy being beloved children of God. Where Lucifer wants us to always want more to be satisfied, Jesus sees that for some people, poverty can end up being the greatest gift because it allows us to love God, not mansions and other luxuries. If we allow Lucifer to convince us that wealth, drugs, alcohol, sensuality, or anything else can be our source of happiness, we make them idols and lose the first line of the Principle and Foundation. We stop praising, worshipping, and serving God and instead fall for the poor substitutes Lucifer offers.

This exercise gets us back to the regular three colloquies. We discuss with Mary how we desire to follow her son, and maybe the attachments that are keeping us from doing so. We then let Mary lead us to her son, where again we state our needs. Finally, we let Jesus and Mary lead us to the Father. This is an important part of our journey into a deeper relationship with Jesus. We are to repeat this exercise two or three times depending on whether we are having four or five prayer periods. Then Ignatius has one more exercise for our final hour of prayer.

Who Are You

To follow God, it is important to see what type of person you are. The first type is all talk but no action. This type knows that they have way more than they need, but never get around to freeing themselves of the possessions they have acquired. Most of their energy is put into struggling to obtain more. They started owning things, and the things ended up owning them. Maybe they started enjoying the odd drink with friends, and now their energies are focused on getting to the next drink. They know they need to stop, and plan to stop, maybe tomorrow, but they probably will not.

The Spiritual Exercises

There are others who have the same good intentions and act on some of them. They want to follow God but on their terms. Yes, they say, I should give more to charity, but rather than asking God where and how much, they may decide on their own what to give and to whom to give it. And we may decide to do more for God—volunteering at church as a reader might be good, and I am there anyway—but what if God wants you to go to a food bank or soup kitchen one day a week. God might want you to connect with the poor you help. You might see further actions you can take to help, but this type just never takes that last step that risks causing a deep conversion. They follow, but just down the street, never following God onto the expressway to see where they might end up.

The followers God wants are those who desire deeply to follow God and to be free to let go of things or keep them, whichever way God calls. Remember the lists of wanting neither health or illness from the Principle and Foundation. God wants us to be free. He knows what we can and cannot do. I am certain God does not want me to play in the NHL, although sixty years ago I would have thought that would be a good thing. I trust God will not ask me to do the impossible, but I ask for the grace to accept the possible things God asks of me. It may not be much, but can we do what is asked? About 30 years ago, I visited, along with several other seminarians, a retired priest whose health was failing. The priest who had taken us asked him what he was doing these days, and he said he prayed a lot. Someone asked him what his prayer was like. He said, "I sit in this chair and start by saying Our Father, and then I begin to think about what that means.

He is not my father, your Father; he is Our Father. All the people in the world are his children. I think of those in Africa, Asia, all his children. The Christians, the Muslims, the Jews. Everyone loved and cared for by God. Then usually after an hour or so I make a coffee." That day that old priest was asked by God to teach some seminarians, and he did what was possible, what God knew he could do. Rest in peace, Fr. Charlie.

With the meditations this day, Ignatius really puts the question to the retreatant: If you say you want to follow Jesus and not be drawn away by Lucifer, what type of follower do you plan to be? Are you getting close to going all in, giving God authority over all your life? Because if the retreatant is ready, there may be costs in this life to that choice. If you are close, Ignatius asks us to discuss in our colloquies any issues where we are resisting letting go of, and even have the courage to ask for poverty if our "things" are keeping us from God.

Decision Making

By this time in the retreat, most retreatants will begin to ponder the questions they may have brought to the retreat. They may be considering vocation choices, changes in their job. A death may have opened issues around change. Very few people would embark on such a long commitment unless they had an important life decision. The retreat has focused on the need to follow Jesus, and it is natural that the retreatant will start to ponder the question that brought them there. For this phase, Ignatius asks the retreatant to focus on just one passage, usually about ten verses, for all five or four

The Spiritual Exercises

prayer periods each day. He gives enough passages that could extend the second week for another eight days. The second week is to look at points in the life of Jesus with the hope of strengthening the retreatant's desire for closeness to God. The director may lengthen or shorten the week.

The retreatant will begin to think about the question they brought during the times he is not praying with the passage of the day. These daily passages are not a Bible study but are meant to help the retreatant fall in love with God and choose to follow. To really follow Jesus one needs humility, and Ignatius sees humility as being on a continuum. Our humility may start with wanting to spend eternity with God and desiring to not do anything that might cut us off from God. As we grow in humility, we move from not wanting to do things against the will of God to actively desiring to do God's will. This is the desire we express each time we pray the Our Father. The deepest form of humility is when we desire to give up all prestige and work humbly to serve the Christ we find in the poor. Ignatius says if we feel called to this level of humility, we should be discussing it with Mary, Jesus, and the Father in our colloquies. This radical humility is what Damien of Molokai lived with the lepers, or what Charles de Foucault lived in the deserts of North Africa. Ignatius encourages us to think about this kind of humility on these days in the second week as we begin to ponder life choices. And the week will progress until it seems like it is time to make decisions. That is when the third week will start.

Now one might wonder what types of choices one would bring to the retreat. It would be good to clarify, with the help of your director, what focused question you wish to bring to God. When choosing a state in life, it is important that we choose what will allow us to best love, praise, and serve God, as well as save our soul. Marriage, religious life, or single life. We can serve and praise God in any of these states. But which one is best suited to the gifts God has given me? The early part of the exercises helped us to seek to be free from attachments that might cloud our decisions. Sometimes we might feel drawn to marriage or religious life by models we see. We choose one. But we should ask ourselves how the gifts we have could be used as a priest or married person to praise, honour, and serve God and make his kingdom visible. A person with perfect pitch will make a better singer or musician than someone who is tone deaf. The retreat has begun to help the retreatant grow in self-knowledge and now, as he comes closer to Jesus, that self-awareness should help in choosing how God is calling.

The first thing Ignatius wants the retreatant to know is that the choice to know God's call will never be sinful. God gives us good options. Choices that go against the will of God or the traditions of the Church are suspect by their nature. The second thing one needs to consider is whether this choice is permanent in nature or may be just for a time. One may be called to work in missionary work. But is that as a vowed religious who dedicates his life to that, or as a lay person with temporary commitments? If one has already made a permanent commitment, then the choice would be to strengthen our commitment. Ignatius does admit, however, that disordered attachments can lead us to commit to something that is not God's call. While he acknowledges this happens, he says if that is suspected, there should be examinations by proper authorities as to the nature of the complicating factors, and discovery if the commitment could be remade freely or maybe abandoned. For non-permanent decisions, Ignatius says we should feel free to move on to new ones with no regrets if our free discernment shows that is God's will. Changes in non-permanent decisions might be made to stay or change within the retreat.

The last instructions regarding decision-making also cover when these decisions might be made. In rare cases, God grants us the grace to know what we should do. There are stories of saints knowing what they should do, but it sometimes happens to ordinary folks. My father went to a dance about eighty years ago. When he got home, he wrote his sister *that* he had met the person he was going to marry. My mother did not have the same insight, but their marriage lasted until his death about forty years ago. For more people, discernment is a longer process, where Ignatius says we need to discern how God is moving our spirits by giving us feelings of consolation and desolation. This is the core of decision-making for Ignatius, and your director will spend time explaining the process, and there are books written on how Ignatius uses these terms. It is one of the biggest insights Ignatius had, and it helps one discern the will of God. I will not try and explain it in a few paragraphs, but if you do experience completing the exercises it will be one of the most valuable skills your director will explain to you. Fleming says it well in *Draw Me into Your Friendship*: "The discernment of spirits which is called for is an entrance into understanding a language of God spoken within our very being."[4]

Sometimes God does not make the decision clear in a flash of insight, or by moments of consolation or desolation. This is not due to failure on our part, but an invitation from God to work it out with logic, pen and paper. It can sometimes take a little longer. We must be very precise with our questions and analysis. But the gift of this kind of decision is we have considered the benefits and drawbacks of both options, and when we move on with our choice, we are clear in our own mind why. This can be helpful if it is a difficult path we are embarking on. It is good to ask God to affirm the decision we have made. There are other techniques. Imagine what advice you might give someone who asked you about the choices. Imagine how you will feel about your choice on your deathbed, or when discussing it with Jesus after you have died.

The second week has the goal of helping the retreatant choose their state of life. The prayer times are simplified: one scripture passage a day prayed with four or five times. The hope is that, especially in the final period each day, the application of the senses will bring our heart closer to the heart of Jesus. The challenges from day five are more in the hours between the prayer periods when we try to clarify our state of life and how will we follow Jesus to best utilize the gifts we have to best praise, worship, and serve God.

New Temptations

In week one we tried to rid ourselves of attachments that were keeping us from having a close relationship with God. Our

The Spiritual Exercises

temptations then might have been tending toward despair. We may have felt at times that we could not be forgiven and freed from our sins, but as we carried on, maybe made a general confession, we began to see that God wants to heal and free us so we can use our freedom to follow God and use the gifts we already have to build the kingdom. The temptation we struggle with in the second week is different. Lucifer may tempt us to try and do too much. Maybe we have some of the first kind of humility and God wants us to move to the second. Here the temptation is not so much "I cannot do it" but "Forget the second kind; I'm going for number three." Of course, if we do not have those gifts, and it is not our call, Lucifer hopes the failure will discourage us from even trying for number two.

Again, just a little note from folks who use FMRI images to study the brain. They say most of our decisions happen before we consciously think about them. Our brains take in various info from our senses and gathers them into one area where we feel good about our life and situation or maybe we feel scared, anxious, or otherwise. By calling us to examine if God is giving us consolations or desolations, Ignatius is trying to help us focus on the early stages of our decisions. By becoming conscious of our emotions, we can make better decisions. By encouraging us to abandon our inordinate attachments that can keep us apart from God, Ignatius is helping us to make a deep attachment to God. In a world with many more distractions than there were around five hundred years ago, his methods are a valuable tool for living.

Enjoy the second week. It is bringing you closer to God and clarifying how you might best follow God. But keep some of what you learned going. Do not stop the examen at noon and in the evening. You might want to review the Principle and Foundation once or twice. You may want to say the Anima Christi sometimes as you get more friendly and familiar with God. Do not forget your colloquies after each prayer. Let a journal be your friend. If you are making these exercises, it is because God called you to receive a gift. Following God is always spiritually valuable:

KEEP YOUR EYE ON THE PRIZE AND HOLD ON.

Third Week

The third week focuses entirely on the Passion. Once again there are variations on how your director may encourage you to live the week. The suggested way is to take it in segments. The first and second prayer periods would cover different passages. Day one, for example, would cover the preparation for the Last Supper and meal itself. The next two prayer periods would be repetitions, and the last one of course would be the application of the senses. Some may wish to break these passages into four parts rather than two, and Ignatius is OK with that. He suggests breaking the Passion into twelve segments and praying with them over six days. The seventh day should be dedicated to the whole Passion, going over it. Maybe stopping longer on certain parts of the story. Each retreatant and director will negotiate how this part of the retreat, focusing on the last days of the life of Jesus, will be lived. Some retreatants may tackle this week in bigger chunks, getting through it all in three or four days. The point is not how you tackle praying about the

Passion. It is more about how the Spirit is touching your soul in the prayer.

It might be good to examine how one has progressed in weeks one and two. In the first week we looked at our sin. We reflected on how our sins had impacted our lives and the lives of those we love and care about. It was not easy. We felt the harm our sins have caused. We also saw that our sins do not have to be the end of the story. We saw how we could bring them to our consciousness with the daily examine and ask for the help of God in developing new habits that were virtuous. We may also have made a general confession and asked for forgiveness. I have heard that Carl Jung, a pioneer in psychotherapy, asked any patients who came to him who were Catholic about their faith practice, and if they had not been to confession for a long time, he told them to go and make a good general confession before he started his therapy. Most found that after the general confession the therapy was not needed. I know myself that I have seen people find healings after making a good confession. This does not always happen. Some disorders benefit from the professional help of a psychiatrist.

In the second week, we tried to come closer to this Jesus who had begun his healing of our sins. We also began to make conscious decisions about how we might follow him. We began to see that following Jesus called for choices; we might have to give up some things and take on other tasks. We began to focus more on our ultimate purpose. Wealth or poverty, health or illness, so many things that we had held as important we now judge as to whether they bring us closer to God. We saw that there was not one way to praise, honour,

The Spiritual Exercises

and serve God, and we struggled to see which path was best suited to our gifts. The daily examinations of consciousness, the colloquies with Mary, Jesus, and the Father, the hours of meditation, being aware of what gave us consolation, what brought desolation, choosing a state of life—all these things have changed us. A retreatant who has lived these weeks well will find themselves changed and their relationship with Jesus much more personal and intense.

Ignatius asks us in this week to finish the work of the first week in a way. As we pray through the Passion, we ask for the grace to see the role our sin played in the Passion. The realization will come that if no one had ever sinned, there would have been no need for redemption. And as small and petty as most of our sins have been, they had a part in Jesus undergoing his Passion. The point is to feel sorrow for our sins, not to give us an excuse to wallow in guilt, but to be motivated to avail ourselves of God's mercy. Tiger Woods worked to discover his golfing sins, worked hard at eliminating them. He developed golfing virtues. As a result, he made millions and grew the audience for golf. His example led other players to get better as well. With the growth in popularity Tiger inspired, the revenues of the PGA grew, and they manage to raise more money annually for charities through their tournament than other professional sports leagues. Correcting our faults can pay huge dividends.

There is one important aspect where Ignatius suggests a change in the prayer each day. While during earlier weeks he suggested each prayer period ends with what he calls the triple colloquy (friendly conversations with Mary, then bringing in Jesus and ending with the Father joining the conversation), during this week Ignatius wants us to really feel the sadness of the Passion and death that Jesus endured for our sake. He wants us to start each day focused on the Passion. He encourages us to keep sombre for the whole day. This is not the week to enjoy a pleasant walk in the sunshine. This week the colloquies might be silent at times. I know when my father was dying of cancer, when his body was wasting away, sometimes I was just with him. Words were not needed, just presence. Sometimes words as well, but often he just wanted me or someone else to be with him. Ignatius suggests that at times this week our colloquy might be just being with Jesus, trying to be with him in the Passion. During moments of extreme joy or pain there are no words that are adequate. But sometimes we need a hand to hold. Ignatius suggests experiencing the Passion, a fragile place, with respect and silence.

In the Catholic tradition, the most familiar memorial acclamation is "Christ has died, Christ is Risen, Christ will come again." Some other traditions stress the resurrection and return more, but in Catholicism, we do not just celebrate Easter—we celebrate the Easter Triduum. We start on Holy Thursday with the Last Supper, Good Friday with the Passion, and only then do we come to Easter. The Gospel of Mark, the earliest and shortest Gospel, has been called a Passion narrative with an introduction, as half the Gospel is about the Passion. The Passion is difficult. The biggest objection that religious Jews had to Jesus being the Messiah was the Passion. Paul proclaimed he preached a Christ crucified, and then said it was a stumbling block for many. It is hard to integrate the Passion into our faith, yet Jesus accepted the Passion. Ignatius has had us come to know Jesus, his love and

The Spiritual Exercises

mercy and invitation to friendship in the first and second weeks. In week three, he challenges us to enter the next level in our relationship with Jesus. Can we experience the Passion with him?

Ignatius really keeps the third week simple. His numbering system for notes and comments go from 91 to 189 for the second week. The third week starts at 190 and ends at 217. He has one instruction that can be difficult but should be followed. He instructs the retreatant while "getting up and dressing to be sad and grieve over such great grief and suffering of Christ our Lord." The retreatant is also instructed to try not to have happy thoughts during the day; even though they are not evil in themselves, he asks that we do not recall them this week. This is a time to remember that Jesus sharing our humanity meant he also shared the human experience of suffering, and this is what we should be recalling this week.

The extent to which one can follow these instructions will determine how this week will be experienced. I have in my life spent time with people dying, sometimes as a priest walking with parishioners and their families at times of great loss or death. Some I have loved deeply. These are often moments of great grace, but the graces are more often seen in hindsight. We need time to just be present to the reality of the suffering, the death. My mother was living with me when she died. After she died, I had to sit at the nurses' station at the hospital just after 1:00 a.m. and call a few family memebers, but I do not remember what I said. Early the next day, I got a call from a retired priest friend who told me he would take any services I had for the next few days. He did not ask me if I wanted him to do that; he told me what he was going to do. He was a wise man, and he knew that I needed some days to be with the grief; I had no need to be going on with life as normal. My mother had died. That was where my mind and heart had to live right then. I would have to re-enter my routines soon enough. But first I had to live the grief. I would see graces. But right then I needed to see the grief. Ignatius asks us to use the skills we have learned in meditation and applying our senses in meditation to try and be with Jesus and the disciples as they lived those last days of his human existence. Remember, the Passion happened before the resurrection, so the disciples did not have the consolation of knowing what was to come. Ignatius knew we might be tempted to flash forward to the resurrection. But if we can live the Passion well, we will be glad we did in the fourth week.

Another note Ignatius makes is to keep doing our daily examens. This too is important to note for two reasons. The first reason is that when we are sad and grieving, we will be less likely to want to spend any time reflecting on our day and how we have been feeling. These examens will help us through the week. The feelings of desolation will be more numerous than feelings of consolation. But this week we will come to appreciate the work we had done to learn to recognize these feelings. The second reason is that while we all feel, we do not always get the benefits of our feelings. We tend to rate our feelings as good or bad. Love is good. Anger is bad. All feelings can bring us good or ill; it is our reactions to them that might be good or bad. Love might not lead to a good result if it is for a neighbour's spouse. Anger may not be bad if it motivates us to stop someone causing harm to another. The sadness and grief of this week will affect us. Examining

The Spiritual Exercises

these feelings, bringing them to our consciousness, help us to channel the energy behind them when praising, glorifying, and serving God.

As mentioned at the start, Ignatius recommends breaking up the Passion into twelve parts and taking two sections a day with repetitions and an application of the senses each day. There could be other ways, but if this is done, you will finish in six days. In chapter one of Genesis, God rested on the seventh day. That is not what Ignatius asks for the seventh day of the third week. Rather than five prayer periods, he invites us to spend all the day thinking about the Passion. How was Mary feeling that day? Or the disciples, what were they thinking? What drove Judas Iscariot to take his life? And how do you feel about the Passion? Are your feelings calling for a response? What will change in your life because Christ died? Christ died for all humanity, but he also died for you—you are part of the humanity he died for. This can be a graced time in the exercises, but also a time of temptation.

The enemy might return at this time to make you feel despair at ever changing. You may feel you could never respond adequately to the love God has shown. One of the most seriously addicted alcoholics I ever met used to manage to quit drinking for Lent every year. But he told me he sometimes had to start again on Good Friday because it was so sad. I have not seen him in over twenty years, but I hope that he received the grace to stop for good one day as his response to the love God showed him on Good Friday. The enemy might also try to tempt as in the second week. We might be tempted to try to do more than God asks, and attempt something we are not capable of accomplishing. Again, our examens and our director can help us respond well to the feelings this week brings.

It is also in week three that Ignatius suggests something I still have not been able to integrate well, an inordinate attachment I struggle with. I have not given up. I know I will succeed, but have not gotten there yet. The area is around food and drink. Now one might wonder why—why, in a week where he only has twenty-seven notes and instructions, are eight of them (210 to 217) about eating and drinking? For one thing, eating and drinking is a part of most of our lives every day we are alive. Many people struggle with alcoholism, obesity, or anorexia. The first twelve-step program was A.A., focusing on alcoholism. It must have been a problem in his day as well, as Ignatius in 211 says in some ways alcohol is easier because you can give it up completely, while you will always have to eat.

And the place he suggests we might start examining our attitudes is the Last Supper. As we meditate on Jesus eating with his disciples, we can begin to see our attitudes toward food as well. He recommends during the week that we keep meals simple, avoiding rich or sweet foods if we can. He encourages us to be moderate even after the retreat, as the daily habits of eating and drinking can become inordinate attachments. Individually and even societally we do not deal well with food. Many in developed countries struggle with obesity or anorexia, while billions are starving each day. I am beginning to realize that attachments to food can damage my relationship with God if I let them be my source of happiness. I remember in the fifties we would feast at Christmas, Easter, and some other special days. But if we feast weekly or more

The Spiritual Exercises

often, we run the risk of inordinate attachments. Maybe we need to cut back. Not to where our health suffers, but maybe we could devote part of our food budget to alleviate hunger in the world. Many stores today make it easy. There is usually a box by the cash registers where you can donate some of the food you purchased on your way to the car. As I said, I am not where I should be around food. Other inordinate attachments have been healed, and I will get there with food as well.

Eating well, not always seeking the best and richest foods, is something each must develop for themselves. Some become vegetarians or vegans. Some might practice fasting or abstinence from meat one day a week. And while I have not accomplished the perfect balance yet, I see the value in keeping it as a goal. Learning how to hold the guitar and keep a steady rhythm improved my playing. And taming other attachments improved my prayer life, so I encourage you to practice moderation around food and drink. And maybe pray for me and others who are not there yet.

It is worth noting that discipline, once learned in one area, can often be transferred to other areas. My mother taught high school and she often had students who played minor league hockey. They had many commitments to practices and travelling to games. She found that since the teams demanded they keep up on their academics, they were diligent students; applying the disciplines they learned playing hockey at a high level could be applied to other areas. I suspect Ignatius thought that if the retreatants could become detached from food, not letting their needs become inordinate, they would learn techniques they could apply in other areas.

I will follow the lead of Ignatius and not say much more about the third week. Each week has been preparation for the fourth week. By the end of this week, the retreatant will have developed a new and more intimate relationship with Jesus. Now they are ready for week four.

The Spiritual Exercises

This crucifix was given to me by a cousin many years ago. I like it because although it depicts the truth of suffering and sacrifice that is part of the journey Jesus calls us to, it also hints at the resurrection; the cross is gone. There is something beyond the cross. Ignatius calls us to look at the cross, but in week four he moves us toward Resurrection. As Helen Reddy sang in "I Am Woman," sometimes wisdom is born from pain.

Fourth Week

The fourth week of the exercises is where Ignatius hopes all retreatants will get to in the end. The previous weeks have been learning skills that have prepared them for this week. As in the third week, there are few instructions (219 to 237). He assumes the retreatant is well versed in his form of prayer by now. Here we are to focus on the resurrection. In week three we were asked to keep our mood sombre, pray in dimly lit chapels, and avoid joyful feelings. Now is the time to step out into the sunlight, see the beauty of creation, laugh, and feel gratitude. Christ is risen. For Catholics, they feel the difference each year as they go to services on Good Friday in a sparse church with no flowers and little music (what music is played is solemn). Then when they return on Easter, the music is joyful, there are flowers, and alleluias ring out. This is the transition Ignatius calls for. While he would not advocate wild excesses around food and drink, there should be no fasting or other penances this week. Christ is risen, alleluia! Where I often go on retreat, groups do the exercises together, and sometimes individuals do the exercises on their own personal schedules. I can usually spot people in week three or week four just by how they are behaving.

The instructions change a bit, of course. He suggests going from five prayer periods to four, or even three. The first day's contemplation is not from the Gospels but has long been speculated on before and since Ignatius. He assumes that the first appearance of Jesus would have been to his mother, Mary. Would not Jesus want to see Mary first after he left the tomb? She welcomed him into her womb. She was the one he met when he left her womb. Would he not want to meet her first? Of course, since there is no scriptural account to start our meditation, the work we have been doing to imagine biblical scenes will be stretched a bit further. How does Jesus look when they meet? Is there something different? He now appears as true God, not true man. In all the resurrection accounts we pray with this week, the task is to see the divinity shining through Jesus, to feel the consolation and peace Jesus brings to those he meets. This should not be a week with many desolations. Let the delight and love that Mary and Jesus have for each other permeate our being. Know that the love and joy he wants for Mary he wants for all humanity. He wants it for you. This is what Ignatius hopes retreatants experience this week.

Ignatius also wants them to have freedom with their colloquies this week. We may want to stick with the usual triple colloquy, or possibly just with one person. Will discussing the meeting with Jesus or Mary be more helpful? One period of prayer may be with Jesus, one with Mary, one with the Father, and after the application of the senses, a group chat. He does not specify any option, trusting the retreatant who

The Spiritual Exercises

has come this far to decide the best option. Ignatius knows any retreatant who has come this far has developed a close relationship with Jesus, and he wants the retreatant to absorb the love Jesus has for them this week.

For the following days, Ignatius recommends prayer periods focus on the resurrection appearance to the ascension. The retreatant has been trying to see Jesus and how he lived on earth, but now the retreat is ending. Now experience the God who is risen. How did Peter feel when he saw Jesus come back asking if Peter loved him? What will you answer as you meet the risen Lord whose death you just contemplated? Will you feed his sheep? How did you experience the meal with Jesus and the disciples he met on the road to Emmaus? Those disciples returned to Jerusalem to share the news. Mary Magdalene became the messenger to the apostles. Who will you announce that Jesus is risen? How will you feel as Jesus ascends into Heaven? You thought he was gone on the cross, but this time he is leaving but will send his Spirit. How will his being with you in this way change you? When retreatants leave after week four, these are questions they might have answered. Most will also know they will never be alone again. During the retreat, they discovered that although they were sinners, they were forgiven sinners. They discovered that there was a call for them to follow Christ and chose to do so. They discovered that Christ did indeed die. They rejoiced that Christ is risen. And when they leave, it will be to prepare for Christ coming again. But not until they complete one last task.

The last exercise is the Contemplation on the Love of God, or the *Contemplatio* if you like Latin jargon. Your director might talk about contemplation versus meditation. Generally, for Ignatius a meditation involves more active work of imagining, where a contemplation would be more passive. The movie *Fiddler on the Roof* tells the story of a couple who see their world ending—their daughters defying traditions for love. At one point, Tevye and Golda are lost in confusion about this thing called love. One of the best duets in the play starts with Tevye asking, "Golda, do you love me?" Golda begins by meditating on the answer; she reflects on their life together for twenty-five years, all that they did as a couple. After much back and forth, Golda decides if what they have done for twenty-five years is not love, what is it, so she supposes she loves him. Tevye supposes he loves her too. They admit it does not change a thing, but after twenty-five years, it's nice to know. They end the meditation and end contemplating this mysterious thing called love. By this point, the retreatant has been thinking about God's love for them and how they can respond in love to God. Now, before they end, Ignatius asks them to rest in God's Love. To contemplate it.

The retreatant is reminded that love is an action and is seen in deeds, not words. It should be remembered that lovers must be able to share with each other. O. Henry wrote a beautiful story called "The Gift of the Magi." A husband pawns a precious watch he inherited to buy a mirror and brushes for his wife, who had beautiful hair. He did not know that she had cut her hair and sold it to a wig maker to buy him a gold chain for his pocket watch. Love calls on us to share. For the prayer, Ignatius asks us to contemplate. Ignatius suggests we imagine ourselves before God and the heavenly hosts and say:

The Spiritual Exercises

> Take Lord, and receive all my liberty
>
> My memory, my understanding, my entire will
>
> All that I have and call my own.
>
> You have given it all to me.
>
> To you, Lord, I return it.
>
> Everything is yours: do with it what you will.
>
> Give me only your love and your grace.
>
> That is enough for me.

You may see in this beautiful prayer the distillation of the ideas Ignatius listed in the Principle and Foundation. There they were ideas, thoughts he was proposing to us. Here they are a simple, heartfelt prayer we make to God. Imagine a couple who meet and feel a certain attraction. They might early on discuss what they hope for in a relationship. As they begin to think of life together, they might discover habits they have that will need to change. As they gradually change to come closer to each other, they disclose to each other the truth of who they are and might even commit to each other. As they begin to see each other as a couple, they begin to realize how each will have to let some of their past die if they are to be able to come together as a couple. And in the end, they may stand before a priest and God and offer themselves to each other. The Contemplation on the Love of God is in some ways our wedding vow to God, a vow we make after spending the retreat coming to know just how much God loves us and wants to spend eternity with us.

Now I should make a little confession of sorts. Although Ignatius planned this for the end of his exercise, that was not where I encountered it. When I started to take my faith seriously once again, I became a regular member of the Newman Centre in Toronto. They had a prayerful community in those days, with committed disciples who saw their faith as demanding much more than showing up for Mass on Sundays. Their music program was incredibly good, and one of the songs they sang was "Take Lord, Receive" by Dan Schutte, SJ. It was a song he wrote for the funeral of a Jesuit mentor, and this song had a lot to do with my journey from working as an accountant to joining L'Arche and eventually the priesthood. It was a part of my personal spirituality long before I even heard of the Spiritual Exercises. Over forty years later, it is still alive in my heart, and the meaning grows richer with each passing year. If I have one hope for my life, it might be that someone might feel my life was lived in such a way that they sing it at my funeral.

In his notes, Ignatius has about 140 supplemental notes that you might hear about if appropriate from your director. I will not go into them, as this is just an invitation to think about the exercises. Ignatius never imagined that most Christians would do these exercises. But he did hope they would do some exercises, even a few mentioned here. I will now look at a few things one might do in the spirit of these exercises to end this little book. Socrates said that an unexamined life was not worth living. I suspect Ignatius believed a faith not examined with these or other exercises was not worth having.

The Spiritual Exercises

This statue I have had for about forty years, and it is called *Family*. But I see it also as an image of the Christian community. The members are all assorted sizes, and they are looking in the same general direction, but they are not all looking exactly in the same direction. Their visions are slightly different, just like us in the Christian community. We are not all the same size or looking *at exactly* the same thing, but we have a common direction.

Spiritual Exercising

Not everyone who does physical exercise is going to train the same way an Olympic athlete would, but there will be some commonalities. There will be repetitions, with some modifications as skills develop. It is the same with spiritual exercising. Do what works, and maybe as you progress, add some more. Parents try to instill spiritual disciplines in their children. I have seen parents teaching children to bless themselves with Holy water as they enter church, not always reminding them that they do it as a reminder that they entered the church through baptism. We bless our food at meals, teach prayers, and maybe when they are a bit older how to recite the Rosary. All of these are spiritual exercises. Let us examine a few.

Now as Vatican II states, the home is the domestic Church. Not even priests spend all their spiritual time in churches, although we spend more time than most in church buildings. What this means is that if we are to begin a regular daily habit of connecting with God, the home is a good place to start. In the Principle and Foundation, Ignatius gives us a clue where to start. Right from the start, we are reminded that we are made to praise, reverence, and serve God. There are many ways we can do that right in our homes, and they can be spiritual exercises, especially if we do them intentionally. When the family gathers for a meal, do they praise God and thank him for the meal? Do they take the time to pray to God and praise him when they wake and thank him for the day before they retire for the night? Many teach these practices to their children, but I am impressed more by couples who continue when the children are grown and leave home. There are many ways we can praise God through the day.

We can make our homes spaces where people can see the reverence we have for God. Some have a crucifix by their main door. When I was younger, most Catholic house in my town had pictures of the Sacred Heart of Jesus and the Immaculate Heart of Mary. Today you might find images of a Divine Mercy icon. There are many beautiful icons people put in their houses. I know one priest who was inspired by Caravaggio, and his rectory is a gallery of reproductions of his religious art. Many have a priest or deacon bless their homes, or even do a ritual with their family where they dedicate their home to God. Statues inside or outside the home of saints or angels tell people the residents revere God. St. Francis started the tradition of Christmas crèches, and they appear in many homes and yards. You can often see some symbols of other faiths that people use to mark their homes as places where God is revered. The home is where we can begin to show reverence to God.

Most of us do our first acts of service in our homes. As Matthew tells us, Jesus said that acts of service done to the least among us are done to himself. At home, children hopefully learn that they are loved by God and by their parents, who see them as precious gifts given to them by God. But they also learn that they can serve their family with grateful hearts for the gifts they have received. Children learn to make beds, wash dishes, take out the garbage, and other chores (especially on a farm). Cutting grass and weeding a garden can be valuable spiritual exercises if done as willing service to Christ. Therese of Lisieux came to see that she was not going to be a missionary, but she could still pray for missionaries and scrub the floors in her convent. Hopefully, you can think of many ways we can learn to praise, reverence, and serve God without ever leaving home. And, if we do, we have begun to lay the foundations of our spiritual journey on solid foundations.

St. Dominic gave the Church the Rosary, partly to help people not in religious life join in the Liturgy of the Hours prayed by priests and religious. As few people were literate, they could not recite the 150 psalms, but 150 Hail Marys was possible. The Spiritual Exercises pick up some of the mysteries. Since the Rosary is strongly scriptural, there is no equivalence to the first week in this prayer. The Joyful Mysteries and the Luminous Mysteries John Paul II added do invite us to think about the events Ignatius would invite us to meditate on in the second week. The Sorrowful Mysteries match up with the third week meditations. Three of the Glorious Mysteries are covered in the fourth week. As you can see, the meditations have overlap with the Spiritual Exercises. There is not the five one-hour prayer periods, or the application of the senses (although you might do that briefly). I know many people who have prayed the Rosary for many years, and it has brought them closer to God. My cousin Fr. Jim Phelan has travelled the world promoting family Rosaries, and he would attest to the value of this prayer. It is an easy prayer form to instruct children because of the repetition.

Another family prayer option might be clearing the table after supper, lighting a candle, reading a short scripture passage, and saying short prayers like an Our Father, Hail Mary, and Glory Be. This can be followed by any prayers of praise, thanksgiving, and petitions people have. This quite simple prayer, one I prayed many years in L'Arche, may not seem to have any connection to Ignatius. I did find that after we had read scripture and quieted ourselves, the spontaneous prayers were in some ways a form of an examination of conscience. Our prayers of praise reminded us of what was going well in our lives, as did the prayers of thanksgiving. The prayers of petition reminded us of what was not working as we asked God to help us do better. I often found this communal form of an examination of conscience helpful.

I have mentioned that twelve-step programs are based roughly on the Spiritual Exercises, although done in a group setting, with group support. The model is not moving into silence for thirty days. People gather with people with similar addictions weekly. Some are in recovery and have been so for a while. Others are trying to stop their addictive behaviours. The new member finds a sponsor, who only promises to say what they have experienced and not be an expert, but a support. There is an acknowledgement of needing a higher power, admitting personal failure, making amends, choosing to do better, and committing to spreading the message.

The Spiritual Exercises

Many parishes have one or two recovering alcoholics leading valuable parish initiatives. The twelve steps have awakened in many people a longing for closeness to God. It is not an accident that many twelve-step groups meet at churches, and it is not just the cheap rent. Many folks have found God and healing in these programs from addictions. Not all do. I have met people who fell off the wagon several times before they had more stable recovery, and they always speak of being in recovery, not being cured. There is great wisdom in that. I have had more than one sin I have had to confess more than once. The advantage of achieving recovery even for a while is that you develop skills to stay in recovery. If you see yourself as completely healed, you let down your guard and relapse. But the twelve steps, while not magic, are a powerful spiritual exercise.

For Catholics, the most powerful spiritual exercise they have is the Mass. Now I never met Ignatius, so I cannot say that the Mass was at the back of his mind as he developed his Spiritual Exercises, but you can see elements of the Mass in them. In the Mass we begin "In the name of the Father, and of the Son, and of the Holy Spirit." Ignatius asks the retreatant to be aware of entering into the presence of God when they enter the space where they will meditate. Four times in the Mass we hear the priest say, "the Lord Be with You." Both in the exercises and the Mass, we should be aware that we are entering into the presence of God in a tangible way. The creed is a sort of Principle and Foundation statement that we remind ourselves of as we begin the Mass, as Ignatius has a similar type of statement at the start of his exercises. We say in the creed that we believe in the forgiveness of sins, and in the penitential rite we recall our sins and ask for forgiveness. Is that not the journey we take spiritually in the first week? In the Liturgy of the Word, especially the Gospels, we hear the story of Jesus, who he is, and hopefully grow in our desire to follow him. Over three years you get to hear all four Gospels, not sequentially, but over many years Catholics get familiar with the story of Jesus. The second week also invites us to ponder parts of that story as well and choose to follow Jesus. The homily and the prayers of the faithful can inspire us to act on our faith, another second-week task. The Church devotes almost one hundred days each year to the seasons of Lent and Easter. Starting on Ash Wednesday all the way through to Pentecost, we focus on themes found in the third and fourth week. And as Ignatius hopes that people leave the exercises as fired-up Intentional Disciples, the mass ends in the Roman missal with the powerful words "Ite, Missa est." Avery Dulles argued years ago that the best translation to English would be "Go, your mission is." He imagined people leaving the Mass to accomplish the mission of Jesus, no songs, no fanfare. I have always regretted it did not happen. But we should remember we come to celebrate Mass to be renewed for our mission of evangelization. Places in the world where people come to communal celebrations are more alive than places where people go to fulfill obligations. The Mass is a wonderful Spiritual Exercise.

The Liturgy of the Hours is a discipline given to priests and religious. Some lay people adopt all or part of it. It is a series of reading from the psalms, non-Gospel scripture passages (the Gospels get prominence in the Mass), and readings from the tradition. The value is found not only in the content

The Spiritual Exercises

but in the discipline of fitting periods of prayer into your daily life. Married couples find it is good to make sure they connect every day and have some longer times together to keep their marriage strong. It is the same with God. It is good to take time for Mass on the weekend, but it is important to find some time each day. I have heard it said that if you know all the psalms and all the works of Shakespeare, you will know every human emotion. Even with a mother who taught high school English and having lived in Stratford for over ten years, I never did get to read all the works of Shakespeare. But going through the 150 psalms every four weeks for years has helped me to cope with my own emotional life, and even occasionally to help others. This used to be an expensive devotion, the four volumes costing several hundred dollars, but apps like Divine Office are more affordable, and if the truth be told much more user friendly. I think the apps have probably led to an uptake in this devotion with the laity.

Now many do not have time every day for Spiritual Exercising. In the spirit of Ignatius, who said to do what you can do well, and do not do what is not possible at present and fail, here are some suggestions:

- Ignatius advised retreatants to be conscious of God as they rose each day and think about what grace they hoped for in the day to come. The first hour in the Liturgy of the Hours is mainly reciting one of psalms, either 95, 100, 67, or 24. You may want to begin your day with one of these psalms. It would only take a moment, but do not get too far into the day without realizing that "This is the day the Lord has made. Let us rejoice and be glad in it."

- You may want to get yourself a small cross or crucifix and wear it every day. It does not have to be visible unless you are a Catholic bishop. As you put it on, thank God for taking up the cross for the world and ask for the grace to accept any crosses you might encounter.

- We are called to acknowledge Christ, try to remember we meet Christ in others. Matthew reminds us that how we treat others is how Jesus will judge us treating him. A wise Jesuit in Colorado advises people to connect with everyone you meet. If it is a friend, mention their name and say something that lets them know you know who they are. If they have been sick, ask how they are doing. If their child got married, ask how the wedding was. You do not have to get a complete history, but saying one or two things can let them know that you know them and care about them. It can be done in a minute or two, but the small talk can have a big effect.

- Friends I know in A.A. stress we need an attitude of gratitude. It is hard to be depressed when you see the things you should be grateful for. In my rural community, you often see bumper stickers that say *If you ate today, thank a farmer*. I also thank God. Gratitude is a choice. It does not matter whether you are rich or poor, your attitude, not your bank account, will determine your happiness. You are who you are and have what you have. Will you choose to praise the Lord? Remember what matters and what doesn't from the Principle and Foundation.

The Spiritual Exercises

- Ignatius said that during the fourth week to get outside and enjoy the world God gave you. Walking in the woods or along a beach can be an important Spiritual Exercise if we go with God. Many Mexicans will say while parting, "*Vaya con Dios.*" Go with God. Vincent Van Gogh struggled at times, but the world came to see the wonders of sunflowers and starry nights that I suspect he saw on walks with God. When I look at works by the Group of Seven, I suspect Algonquin Park was a cathedral in their eyes.

- Spend time in the rough edges of society. If the Lord hears the cry of the poor, we as Intentional Disciples should hear that cry as well. I may have meditated and contemplated God in seminaries and retreat house. I met God in L'Arche, in the rainforests of Nicaragua, in the streets of Toronto, and in many other places I did not need a suit to feel comfortable in. If you can experience the wonder of giving love to others, you will meet God. Remember the non-biblical story of the fourth magi. He gave away his gifts on the road and never got to see Jesus in the manger. But he was the magi that Jesus called to be with him on calvary. There may be little history in this story, but there is truth.

- For me the most important part of the exercise you should include in your daily life is the examen. Take time if you can around noon and in the evening to review the past few hours. Start with what you are grateful for. Ask God to see your day with God's help and eyes. Were there moments you felt you were with God? Were there times you were not in sync with God (what some would call sin)? Ask for forgiveness where it is needed. Resolve to change the places you slipped, and maybe think of amends you can make. Most days fifteen minutes can accomplish this task. Even if you just do it in the evening it can help. People who are in love want to call or visit each other every day. They keep track of whether the contacts are growing in frequency. They would see this as a pleasant time, as they see it helping the relationship grow. Why do we resist keeping track of how we are growing closer to God?

- Related to this is one of the ways Ignatius helps us abandon vice and grow on virtue. If we feel we watch too much TV, we might decide to pray or go for a walk more often. We could take our Daily Examen time to record how many thirty-minutes periods we watch TV each day and make a list. We could also list how many times we took a thirty-minute walk or prayed. Psychology has shown that simply tracking behaviours is a simple way to change them.

I could go on. Daily Rosaries, weekday Masses, volunteering at a food bank or soup kitchen. Maybe volunteer to drive seniors, join a mission trip to build a school, or dig a well in a developing country. There are many things you could do. Be aware that your temptation might be to think you cannot change, or to try to do too much too quickly (review temptations in the first and second week). I had a friend who never helped at church although she attended weekly. Her father had been a super volunteer and his family suffered because he was always working at the church. It was only in her fifties she

The Spiritual Exercises

could start volunteering. Use wisdom in starting or changing spiritual practices.

If there is anything I hope from these reflections it is that as you become familiar with the spiritual journey Ignatius went on, you might see God acting in your life and become more conscious of the Divine presence. I am finishing up these pages in the twenty-third week of Ordinary Time in the Catholic Liturgical year. Ignatius helps me understand the prayers of the Church, in this and most weeks. The Gospel on Sunday had difficult passages about loving Jesus and hating mother and father, as well as making sure you can finish a house you start and win a war because you have the resources. Now we know Jesus said loving God and loving neighbour were the two great commandments, but Ignatius teaches in the Principle and Foundation and in the *Contemplatio* that loving God must be our primary love, before all others. Of course, if we love God, we love who and what God loves, which includes our families. The temptation of the second week is to take on what we cannot complete, so of course we do not start a building project or a war if we do not have the resources to finish.

In the Office of Readings on Wednesday there is a beautiful reading from Habakkuk 2:4b–20. He is really pointing out the people's faults, and in the last section he mocks them for praying to wood and stone idols and expecting to get wisdom from them. He says go ahead and cover them with gold and silver, they will not breathe and speak to you. Instead, go to God's temple and sit in silence. Then you will encounter God, a sentiment Ignatius would endorse. The reading for midday prayer has Paul's great line: "Love never fails." This reading again draws me back to the *Contemplatio*. The exercises over the years have given me a way to pray and a framework to interpret my walk with God. If my ramblings help anyone else see God in their lives, I am glad. If not, I still praise and thank God for helping me draw closer to him because of some reflections Ignatius had in a cave in Manresa five hundred years ago

Acknowledgements

Before I start, I give a nod to those who goaded me on to search for God using exercises developed in a cave in Spain by Ignatius of Loyola. These writings changed his life and the lives of others, including myself. The first evidence I saw of the existence of a Jesuit Spirituality was when I encountered the works of Bernard Lonergan, and Karl Rahner's book on prayer, *Encounters with Silence*. These two authors piqued my curiosity, and when I began to contemplate the priesthood, they were probably the reason that I explored becoming a Jesuit. Although I never did join the Jesuits, several Jesuits played key parts in my coming to understand these exercises. The biggest influences were Bill Addley, Larry Gillick, Bill Clarke, Bill German, Dick Dunphy, and Ed Kinerk. Some of the priests from the Diocese of London also helped along the way, principally Jack O'Flaherty, Michael Prieur, and Greg Blonde.

In addition, I am very grateful to some who read earlier drafts of this book: Fr. Peter Poel, Dr. Chris Carreira, C. Psych, Fr. Ed Kinerk, Gail Donohue Storey, and Bob and

Darlene Daudin. Their reading and comments encouraged me to continue working on the text. My family was the "domestic Church" where I first encountered God, and I am grateful to have lived in a family and community that had a reverence for God while I was growing up. That formation allowed me to recognize it when God finally made an appearance in my life.

Lastly, I thank God for developing the relationship with me that I have today. I may never understand God any more than a newborn understands who its parents are, but just as the newborn discovers that they are loved by their parents, I have discovered I am loved by God. I may have discovered a few things about God, as I did about my parents, but I do not need to understand how God made the universe, and I wish the astrophysicists well as they try to figure out what happened in three crucial minutes almost 14 billion years ago. I am happy to just know I am loved by God, and he offers me guidance from time to time. And in the end, of the many blessings I am grateful for, this is the one I appreciate the most.

NOTES

1. Flemming. David L: Draw me into Your Friendship. The Instiyute of Jesuit Sources, 1996. Page3

2. Flannery, Austin. O.P., Editor: Vatican II;The Conciliar and Post Concilliar Document. Study Edition. Lumen Gentium (11) Page 305. See Also Cathechism of the Catholic Church (Nos. !324;1327).

3. Flemming (23) Page 26

4. Flemming(176) Page 139

Printed in Canada